Landscapes of
CYPRUS

a countryside guide
Ninth edition

Geoff Daniel
revised and updated by
Mark George and Jane Mead

SUNFLOWER BOOKS

Ninth edition
Copyright © 2023
Sunflower Books™
P O Box 36160
London SW7 3WS, UK

All rights reserved.
No part of this publication
may be reproduced, stored
in a retrieval system, or
transmitted by any form
or by any means, electronic,
mechanical, photocopying,
recording or otherwise,
without the prior written
permission of the publishers.

Sunflower Books and
'Landscapes' are
Registered Trademarks.

ISBN 978-1-85691-548-9

Cyprus lacemakers

Important note to the reader

We have tried to ensure that the descriptions and maps in this book are error-free at press date. Travellers to Cyprus will be aware of changes to the names of major towns and cities — Lefkosia for Nicosia, Lemesos for Limassol. This is part of official moves to create a stronger national identity in the Greek part of the island. We have incorporated the major changes, but you will no doubt encounter others. The book will be updated, where necessary, whenever future editions permit. It will be very helpful for us to receive your comments (sent to info@sunflowerbooks.co.uk, please) for the updating of future editions and for our online update service.

We also rely on those who use this book — especially walkers — to take along a good supply of common sense when they explore. Conditions change fairly rapidly on Cyprus, and ***storm damage or bulldozing may make a route unsafe at any time***. If the route is not as we outline it here, and your way ahead is not secure, return to the point of departure. ***Never attempt to complete a tour or walk under hazardous conditions!*** Please read carefully the notes on pages 19 and 42 to 49, as well as the introductory comments at the beginning of each tour and walk (regarding road conditions, equipment, grade, distances and time, etc). Explore **safely**, while at the same time respecting the beauty of the countryside.

Cover photograph: Petra tou Romiou (Rocks of Aphrodite, Car tour 2)
Title page: in the Troodos Mountains

Photographs: 25 (top), 30 (top), 89 (top left), 99 (bottom), 119: John and Christine Oldfield; 33, 37, 39, 63 (top), 114, 130, cover: istock photo; 17, 29 (bottom right), 55, 75 (top), 76-7, 77 (top), 99 (top), 102 (bottom): Sunflower Books; 58, 68 (top), 91: Mark George; 30-1, 54, 61, 65, 70-1, 80-1, 110-1, 113: Shutterstock; all other photographs: the author
Maps and plans: Sunflower Books
Drawings: Katharina Kelly
A CIP catalogue record for this book is available from the British Library.
Printed and bound in England: Short Run Press, Exeter

Contents

Preface	5
Acknowledgements; Books	6
Getting about	7
Plans of Lefkosia, Pafos, Larnaka, Lemesos, Agia Napa	8
with exits for motorists, bus and service taxi locations	
Picnicking	14
Picnic suggestions	15
A country code for walkers and motorists	19
Touring	20
WESTERN WAYS (Tour 1)	22
Pafos • Coral Bay • Pegia • Kathikas • Drousseia • Prodhromi • Lakki • Baths of Aphrodite • (4WD options) • Polis • Skoulli • Stroumbi • Pafos	
OLD VILLAGES, ROCKS AND BONES! (Tour 2)	26
Pafos • Geroskipou • Kouklia • Pano Arkhimandrita • Dhora • Arsos • Omodhos • Episkopi • Kourion • Petra tou Romiou • Pafos	
LAND OF THE MOUFFLON (Tour 3)	28
Pafos • Polemi • Kannaviou • Stavros tis Psokas • Dhodheka Anemi • Cedar Valley • Kykko Monastery • Panagia • Chrysorroyiatissa Monastery • Statos • Pafos	
FROM PAFOS TO PLATRES (Tour 4)	32
Pafos • Asprokremnos Dam • Nikouklia • Phasoula • Agios Georgios • Kithasi • Kedhares • Agios Nikolaos • Pera Pedi • Saittas • Platres	
A CAPITAL CIRCUIT (Tour 5)	34
Lemesos • Trimiklini • Platres • Troodos • Kakopetria • Galata • Peristerona • Lefkosia • (Stavrovouni Monastery) • Lemesos	
THE HEIGHT OF ORTHODOXY (Tour 6)	37
Larnaka • Hala Sultan Tekke • Kiti • Dhromolaxia • Kalokhorio • Pyrga • Stavrovouni Monastery • Kophinou • Larnaka	
THE FAR EAST (Tour 7)	39
Larnaka • Dhekelia crossroads • Phrenaros • Dherinia • Paralimni • Protaras • Cape Greco • Agia Napa • Xylophagou • Larnaka	
Walking	42
Grading, waymarking, maps, GPS	42
Where to stay	44
Weather	45
What to take	45
Walkers' checklist	46
Nuisances	47

4 Landscapes of Cyprus

Photography	47
Greek for walkers	48
Organisation of the walks	48
THE WALKS (● see explanation of symbols on page 42)	
1 Rounding Mount Olympos	50
2 Makrya Kontarka	53
3 Troodos • Kaledonia Falls • Platres	55
4 Almyrolivado and Kambos tou Livadiou	58
5 Pouziaris Nature Trail	60
6 Trooditissa	62
7 Madhari Ridge	64
8 Circuit from Pera Pedi	67
9 Stavros tis Psokas	69
10 Cedar Valley and Mount Tripylos	72
11 Circuit from Agios Neophytos	74
12 Around Kathikas	76
13 Kissonerga to Coral Bay	78
14 Lara Beach	80
15 From Drousseia to Agios Georgios	84
16 Avagas Gorge Circuit	85
17 Khapotami Gorge	87
18 Circuit from Alekhtora	91
19 Fontana Amorosa coastal trail	94
20 The 'Aphrodonis' Trail	96
21 Akamas gold	99
22 Two Akamas villages	101
23 Miliou • Theletra • Miliou	103
24 Agios Georgios Alamanou to Governor's Beach	106
25 From Kellaki to Phinikaria	108
26 Mount Makheras	113
27 Stavrovouni Monastery	116
28 Around Cape Kiti	118
29 Agia Napa • Cape Greco • Protaras	121
30 Agia Napa to Profitis Ilias	125
Service taxi and bus timetables	127
Index	135
Fold-out island map	*inside back cover*

Lakki harbour

# Preface

Cyprus, birthplace of the mythical love goddess Aphrodite, yields its greatest pleasures to the visitor who makes an effort towards closer acquaintance.

If you are content with sun, sand, surf and soured brandy, then you won't be disappointed. But deeper exploration of this special island, on foot or on wheels, coupled with a healthy curiosity about its people and its traditions, will reward you with experiences to treasure for a lifetime. Should your first visit to Cyprus be the start of an incurable love affair, do not be at all surprised!

This Ninth edition of *Landscapes of Cyprus* is divided into three main sections, each with its own introduction.

For **motorists**, there are car tours taking in lively resorts, picturesque villages, mountain spectacle, fast new roads and very slow old ones. There are suggestions for 4WD enthusiasts, too.

Picnickers can take their choice of authorised sites with benches and barbecue facilities, or out-of-the-way locations along the route of a walk.

Walkers have a comprehensive guide to Cyprus on foot, covering most areas of the island. Most of the walks are within the stride of anyone sound in wind and limb, and most are easily accessible. The book was totally revised, with almost all routes rewalked, for the Eighth edition (2019). Unfortunately, due to the pandemic, we were unable to rewalk all routes for this edition, and have had to base revisions on updates from users.

Cyprus — past

The turbulent history of Cyprus dates back to the Stone Age, and the island has undergone numerous changes of 'ownership' over the centuries. Turks, Romans, Greeks, Venetians, and the British have all played a part in the island's destiny. In Lefkosia the Cyprus Museum and the Museum of National Struggle are well worth visiting to gain an appreciation of the past.

Throughout the island, richly historic sites beckon the curious traveller, not least the imposing 13th-century castle at Kolossi, Lefkosia's Venetian walls, the ancient Tombs of the Kings at Pafos, and the Neolithic settlement at Khirokitia.

In the mountainous Troodos region, nine churches on UNESCO's World Heritage list are rightly famous for beautiful frescoes painted between the 11th and 15th centuries.

Cyprus — present
Cyprus has been an independent republic within the British Commonwealth since 1960, joining the EU in 2004. In 1974 Turkey occupied the northern and northeastern regions (some 36% of the island; see the fold-out map), establishing a state which remains unrecognised in the international community. For the past decade, however, it has been possible to travel freely between the two sectors: see pages 20-21. While *Landscapes of Cyprus* regrettably confines its coverage to the south of the still-divided island, those wishing to enjoy the best walks in the north can do so with Sunflower's PDF guide *Walk & Eat North Cyprus* — while sampling delicious food along the way.

Cyprus — people
For all their upheavals, Greek Cypriots remain among the most cheerful, gregarious and hospitable folk you could ever meet. English is widely understood, but even a stumbling attempt at a few words of Greek (see page 48) on the part of the visitor is warmly appreciated. Cypriot hospitality is legendary — *kopiaste!* (come in and join us!) — and should always be accepted, even if sparingly.

Cyprus — environment
Walking, and other leisure activities which respect the island's somewhat fragile environment, will become increasingly important as conventional coast-based tourism heads towards saturation point. The creation of a national park in the beautiful Akamas region in the west was a positive move to ensure protection of sensitive areas such as the green turtle nesting grounds at Lara Beach.

Acknowledgements
My thanks to various Sunflower authors and the Sunflower team for revising earlier editions of the book, but particularly to Mark George and Jane Mead who rewalked most of the routes for both the Seventh and Eighth editions, as well as contributing some new walks. *Do* visit their website for even more island walks: www.cypruswalks.net.

Books
Landscapes of Cyprus is a guide to countryside exploration, intended to be used in addition to a general guide. Christos Georgiades' *Nature of Cyprus — environment, flora and fauna*, available on the island, is a valuable pictorial reference; Colin Thubron's *Journey into Cyprus*, an account of a pre-1974 walk round the island, is a scholarly but absorbing read; and Lawrence Durrell's classic, *Bitter Lemons,* is an amusing and poignant portrait of a Cyprus long gone. To discover the best walks and tours in northern Cyprus, see Sunflower's *Walk & Eat North Cyprus.*

Getting about

A **hired car** is undoubtedly the most practical way of exploring Cyprus. Numerous companies offer a wide range of vehicles, from runabouts to prestige models. Small 4WD soft-tops are very popular, and their modest extra cost is worth considering if you plan trips into the mountains or remote regions — such is the rough condition of many minor road surfaces. I have included some 4WD route suggestions in this book.

Coach tours operate from the main tourist centres, and offer a painless introduction to road conditions and a comfortable view of island scenery.

Intercity buses are an inexpensive way of moving from one place to another, perhaps for tackling a walk out of a different centre from your hotel base.

Taxis operate in profusion in the towns, more sparsely in villages, and all are identified by a prefix 'T' to the registration number. Rates are fixed by the authorities, and urban taxis are obliged to operate a meter on all journeys. Fares are not high, but on longer journeys it is wise to agree a price in advance. In town you will likely ride in a new Mercedes, but in a village it will probably be something older and more interesting!

Service taxis are a useful way of getting from town to town if you're not in a hurry. They ply between major centres approximately every half-hour and will pick you up at your hotel and take you anywhere central at your destination, picking up and dropping off other passengers en route. They are useful on walks which end on a service taxi route: just ask a bar or café owner to request a taxi stop on its next run. Rates are very cheap for the service offered. You will share your trip with other passengers (possibly in a minibus), but this is the only inconvenience.

Local buses are usually not very helpful for the walker; essentially they bring village folk to town in early morning and take them home later in the day.

Service taxi and bus timetables are given on pages 127-134, but ***do collect an up-to-date timetable*** from the nearest tourist office as soon as you arrive on Cyprus or, better still, log on to **www.cyprusbybus.com** before you go, where you can search all local and intercity bus routes, bus stops and timetables by area, with interactive maps.

8 Landscapes of Cyprus

LEFKOSIA (Nicosia)

1. Information
2. Post Office
3. Municipal Library
4. Town Hall
5. Municipal Museum (of History)
6. Museum of the National Struggle
7. St John's Cathedral
8. Archbishop's Palace and Makarios Cultural Centre
9. Municipal Cultural Centre
10. Police Station
11. Cyprus Archaeological Museum
12. Telephones
13. Municipal Theatre
14. House of Representatives
15. Hospital
16. British High Commission
17. Cyprus Airways
18. US Embassy
19. Presidential Palace
20. Liberty Monument
21. Bayraktar Mosque
22. Museum of Contemporary Art
23. Omeriye Mosque
24. Trypioti Church
25. Chrysaliniotissa Church/ Crafts Centre
26. Faneromeni Church
27. Ledra Palace

🚗 Travel & Express (Cyprus Interurban Taxi Co — Service Taxis)

🚌 Bus 'Station' (Solomos Square)

🟥 Crossing Points for North Cyprus

Plan of Lefkosia 9

10 Landscapes of Cyprus

PAFOS (Paphos)
1. Tourist Information
2. Cyprus Airways
3. Market
4. Police Station
5. Stadium
6. Library
7. Markedeio Theatre
8. Town Hall
9. Telephones
10. Bishop's Palace
11. Byzantine Museum
12. Ethnographical Museum
13. Post Office
14. Agia Solomoni Catacomb
15. Ruined Theatre
16. Odeon and Agora
17. Aquarium
18. Frankish Baths
19. Dionysos Houses (Mosaics)
20. Byzantine Fortress
21. St Paul's Pillar
22. Early Basilica (Ruins)
23. Customs House
24. Pafos Castle
25. Medieval Fort (Ruin)

🚗 Travel & Express (Interurban Taxi Co Service Taxis)
🚌1 Karavella Bus Station
🚌2 Kato Pafos Bus 'Station'

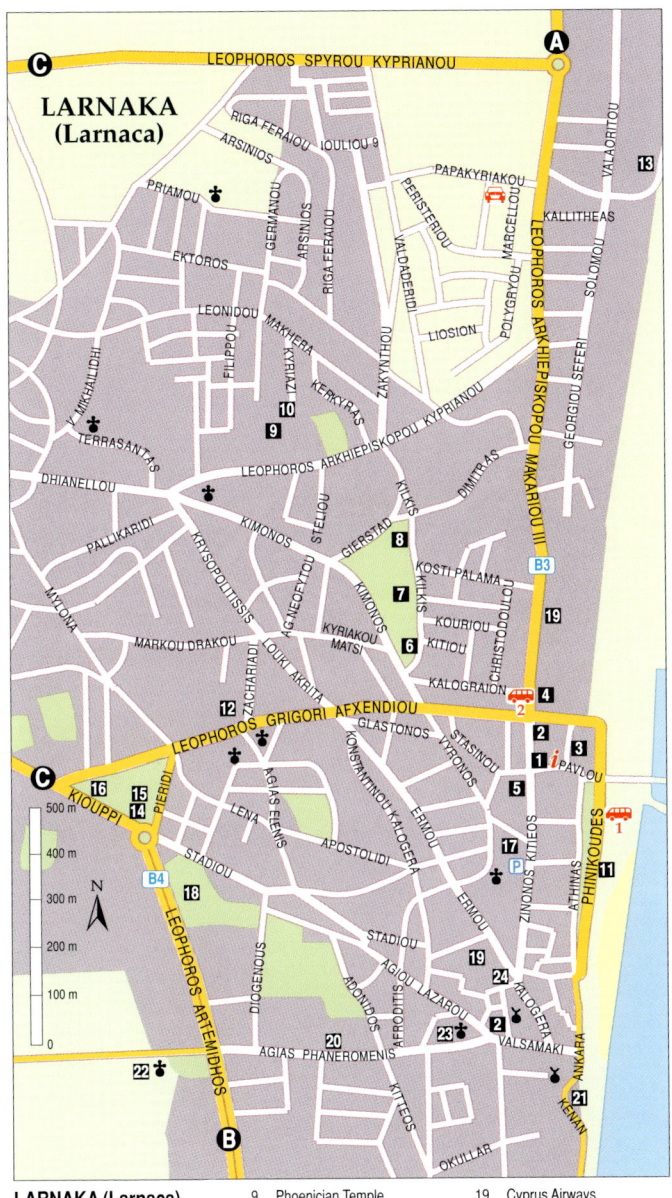

LARNAKA (Larnaca)
1. Tourist Information
2. Post Office
3. Municipal Cultural Centre
4. Police Station
5. Pierides Museum (Archaeology)
6. Archaeological Museum
7. Acropolis of Kition
8. Tennis Courts
9. Phoenician Temple
10. Mycenean Walls
11. Kimon Statue
12. Hospital
13. Customs Office
14. Municipal Theatre
15. Natural History Museum
16. Municipal Library
17. Telephones
18. Stadium
19. Cyprus Airways
20. Cultural/Sports Centre
21. Medieval Fort (Museum)
22. Agia Phaneromeni
23. Agios Lazarus
24. Market

🚗 Travel & Express (Interurban Taxi Co — Service Taxis)
🚌 1 Bus 'Station' (Phinikoudes)
🚌 2 Osea buses

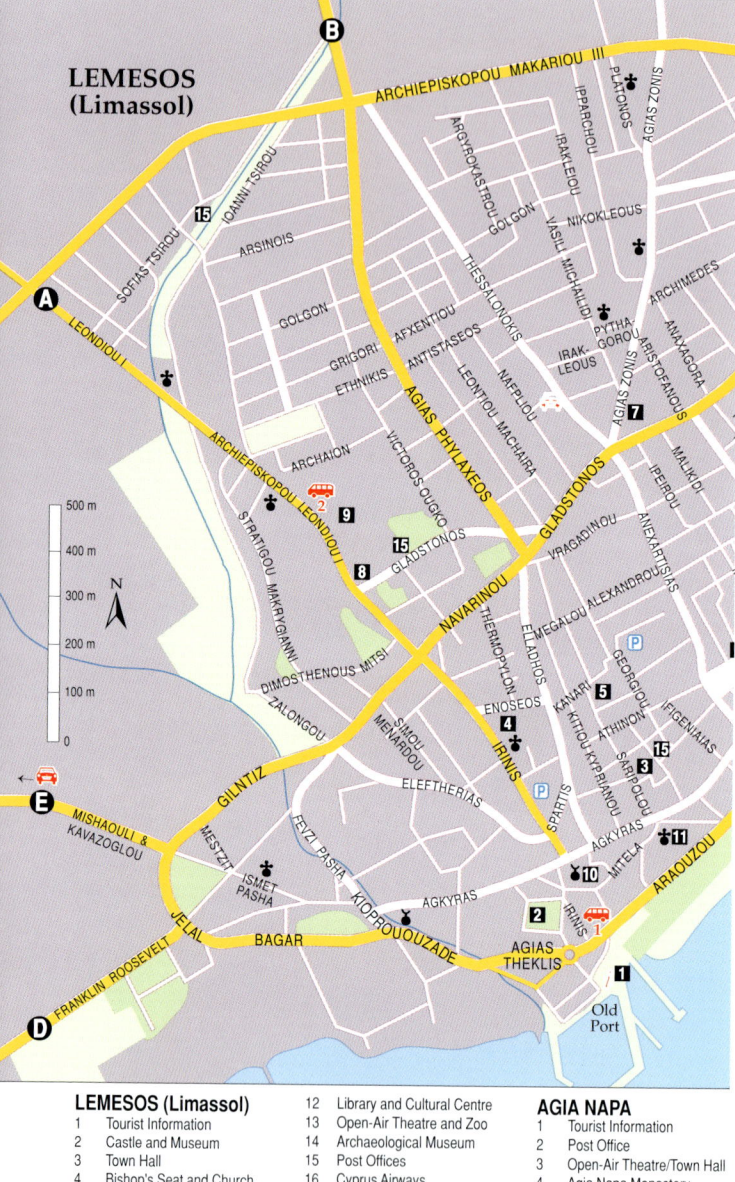

LEMESOS (Limassol)
1 Tourist Information
2 Castle and Museum
3 Town Hall
4 Bishop's Seat and Church
5 Market
6 Telephones
7 Municipal Theatre
8 Police Headquarters
9 Hospital
10 Great Mosque (Kebir)
11 Cathedral
12 Library and Cultural Centre
13 Open-Air Theatre and Zoo
14 Archaeological Museum
15 Post Offices
16 Cyprus Airways
17 Art Museums
🚐 Travel & Express (Interurban Taxi Co — Service Taxis)
🚌1 Intercity Buses
🚌2 EMEL Central Station
🚌3 to EMEL Lambrou Porfira Station (650m/yds)

AGIA NAPA
1 Tourist Information
2 Post Office
3 Open-Air Theatre/Town Hall
4 Agia Napa Monastery
5 Police Station
6 Municipal (Sea) Museum
🚌1 Intercity Bus Stop
🚌2 Osea Bus Stop

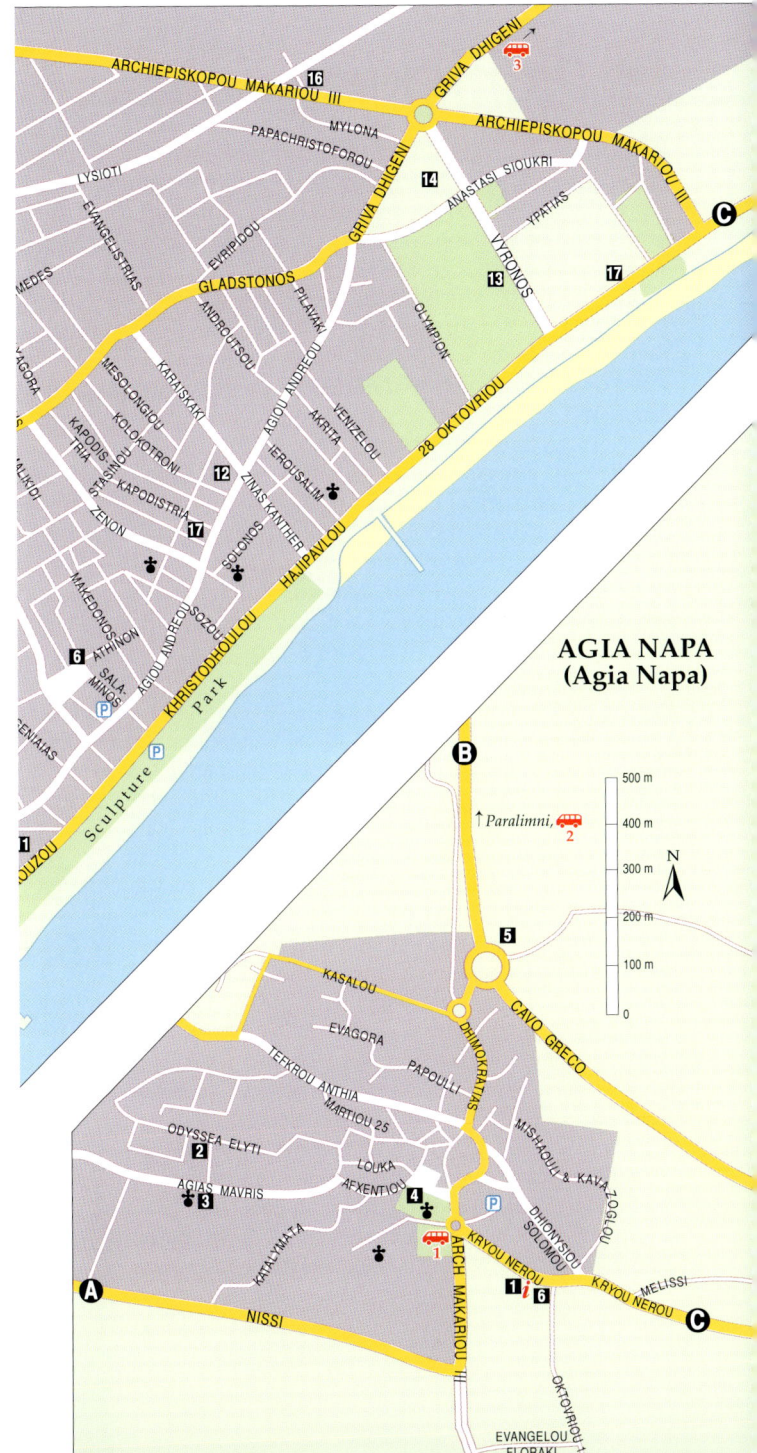

Picnicking

Picnicking is great fun on Cyprus, not least for Cypriots themselves, who will happily tuck into an outdoor feast, especially at weekends or on festival days. This enthusiasm does not extend to walking for pleasure, however, so you are most likely to come across groups of local families enjoying an outing at an official site which is easily accessible by car.

Such a site might suit your requirements — or you may prefer to seek out somewhere much more secluded along the route of a walk. Much of the island is open countryside, but it is a matter of common sense and courtesy not to picnic within any obvious fencing or boundary.

Official sites: The Cyprus Tourism Organisation and Forestry Department have established about 40 sites. Many of them are concentrated in the Troodos mountain region, but there are excellent sites dotted all around the island. The best sites offer car parking, toilet facilities, drinking water, tables and benches, barbecue facilities and play areas for children. At some of the smaller sites in less visited areas, facilities might be minimal. Official sites are indicated in the car touring notes and on the fold-out touring map by the symbol (⌐). Remember that in winter and early spring many will be inaccessible, since they lie along rough mountain roads. A leaflet describing all these sites and a few official camp sites (the only places where camping is allowed) is available from tourist information centres on the island.

Alternative suggestions: If you prefer a picnic 'away from it all', or if you find official sites crowded (likely at weekends and in high summer), you could picnic along the route of one of the walks in this book.

All the information you need to get to one of these 'private' picnics is given on the following pages, *where picnic numbers correspond to walk numbers*, so that you can quickly find the general location by looking at the pull-out touring map (on which the area of each walk is shown in green within a white circle). I include transport details (🚌: how to get there by bus; 🚗: where to park if you come by car or taxi), how long a walk you'll have *each way*,

Lara Beach (Picnic 14)

Picnic suggestions 15

and views or setting. Beside the picnic title you'll find a map reference: the exact location of the picnic spot is shown on this *walking* map by the symbol **P**. Finally, to help you choose the right setting, many of the picnic spots are illustrated.

Please remember that these 'alternative' picnic places are generally off the beaten track: you will need to wear sensible shoes and almost certainly a sunhat (the symbol ○ at the right of a picnic title indicates a *picnic place in full sun*).

If travelling to your picnic by service taxi or bus, please be sure to collect an up-to-date transport timetable with operators' telephone numbers from a tourist information office or download one in advance of your visit.

If travelling to your picnic by hired car, watch out for animals and children on country roads and drive especially carefully through narrow village streets. Do park well off the road — without damaging plants; *never* block a road or track.

All picnickers should read the country code on page 19 and go quietly in the countryside.

1 MOUNT OLYMPOS (map pages 56-56, Troodos photos on pages 1, 51 and 61)

by car: 45min on foot   *by bus: 45min on foot*
🚗: park as for Walk 1 on page 50.
🚌: to/from Troodos; recheck times, and make sure there is a suitable return!
From Troodos, follow Walk 1 along the Atalante Trail for the first 3km, to an open area where there are numerous picnicking possibilities in pleasant surroundings and with extensive views. On the Artemis Trail (the Alternative walk) there are also plenty of benches with stunning views where picnics can be enjoyed.

16   Landscapes of Cyprus

2 MAKRYA KONTARKA (map pages 56-57, photo on page 53)

by car: 15-50min on foot *by bus: 15-50min on foot*

🚗 and 🚌: as for Picnic 1.

From Troodos, take the Persephone Nature Trail from the southern end of the main street as described in Walk 2 for 15 minutes, to the group of benches among tall pines shown on page 53. This is a cool spot, but a picnic at the end of the trail (Makrya Kontarka; 50min), with magnificent views, is highly recommended, although there is little shade.

3 KALEDONIA FALLS (map pages 56-57, photos on page 54 and 55)

by car: 5-45min on foot *by bus: about 1h10 on foot*

🚗: park near the signposted Kaledonia Falls Nature Trail, by the side of a rough road that leads from a point northwest of Psilon Dhendron (see map for car symbol). From here it's a five minute walk to the falls. Or park at the trout farm and follow the trail up to the falls, or find a suitable place to sit beside the Kryos River within a shorter distance.

🚌: to/from Platres and walk uphill to Psilon Dhendron to begin

Shady trees, pleasant ferns; very crowded in season and at weekends!

4 ALMYROLIVADO/KAMBOS TOU LIVADIOU/MESAPOTAMOS (map pages 56-57)

by car: up to 10min on foot *by bus: not practical*

🚗: park at one of the sites on the B9 east of Troodos (Car tour 5) or at Mesapotamos Monastery. Although it is not on the route of Walk 4, Mesapotamos *is* worth a visit; take the signposted dirt road east of Psilon Dhendron.

These are wooded, shady settings. There are organised sites, but 'unofficial' settings nearby — lovely places to stroll.

5 ABOVE PSILON DHENDRON (map pages 56-57, photo on page 55)

by car or taxi: 6min on foot *by bus: 30min on foot*

🚗 to Psilon Dhendron or 🚌 to Platres (see Picnic 3) and walk uphill to Psilon Dhendron

Follow Walk 5 for 6min, to a bench set on a rise to your right. Lovely views down to Platres and the trout farm and up to the mountains; ample shade.

7 MADHARI RIDGE (map pages 64-65, photo on page 66)

by car: 15-40min on foot *by bus: not practical*

🚗: park near the start of the nature trail described in Walk 7.

From the nature trail information board, climb to the bench at the 15min-point for superb views over Kyperounda village; or follow Walk 7 for about 40 minutes, to the clearing with views over the Mesaoria Plain and towards Mount Adelphi.

8 PERA PEDI (map page 67)

by car: just 1min on foot *by bus: not practical*

🚗: park in Pera Pedi

Follow Walk 8 to the Kryos River; a lovely peaceful area has been created, with benches, plenty of shade and the sound of running water.

10 MOUNT TRIPYLOS (map and nearby photo on page 73)

by car: 40min on foot *by bus: not accessible*

🚗: park at the Dhodheka Anemi junction (the 55km-point in Car tour 3, page 28), or park at Cedar Valley.

See Walk 10, page 72: it's 2.5km to the top of Mount Tripylos from Dhodheka Anemi, 2km from the picnic area at Cedar Valley. The ascent is the same from both (about 250m/820ft). There's a fire-watch station at the peak, and a small picnic area in a lovely setting.

Picnic suggestions 17

12 KATHIKAS SPRING (map page 77, photo page 25)

by car: 20min on foot   *by bus: not practical*
🚗: park at Kathikas (the 27km-point in Car tour 1).
Follow Walk 12 to the 20min-point. This is a tranquil setting with a shady bench and a spring (operate the pump by a handle on the right).

13 MAVROKOLYMBOS DAM (map and nearby photo on page 79)

by car: up to 15min on foot   *by bus: not practical*
🚗: park near the dam, on the Akoursos road (signposted off the main Pafos–Coral Bay road).
You'll find ample quiet spots on the banks of this irrigation reservoir.

14 LARA BEACH (map pages 82-83, photo on pages 14-15) ○

by car or boat: up to 10min on foot   *by bus: not accessible*
🚗: park at Lara Beach or take a ⛵ from Pafos (see Walk 14, page 80).
A quiet undeveloped beach with a single, seasonal café.

18a ALEKHTORA VALLEY VIEWS (map page 93) ○

by car: no walking or up to 45min on foot   *by bus: not practical*
🚗: park well off the road near the 'Alekhtora' sign and fruit packing factory at the start of Walk 18 (page 94) — or park further up the track.
Follow Walk 18 to the 45min-point (some picnickers drive most of the way). Go up on to the antenna platform and walk 50m past the antenna. Choose a spot on the right — on the grass or the rocks — overlooking the valley. No shade.

18b KHAPOTAMI GORGE OVERLOOK (map page 93) ○

by car: up to 1h08min on foot   *by bus: not practical*
🚗: park as for Picnic 18a above.
Follow Walk 18 to the 1h10min-point, at the edge of the rocky terracing. As long as you don't mind dodging the goat droppings, this is a spectacular site. No shade.

20 'APHRODONIS' TRAIL (map on reverse of touring map, photos on pages 96-97 and 99)

by car   *by bus and taxi: up to 1h10min on foot*
🚗: park near the restaurant at the Baths of Aphrodite.
🚌 from Pafos to Polis; then bus or taxi to the Baths
There are numerous lovely spots on the first, shared part of the two trails; the benches at trail point 11 (35min) are ideal, as is the shady hollow by Pyrgos tis Rigaenas (1h10min).

21 SMIGIES (map on reverse of touring map, photo below)

by car: no walking, or up to about 2h on foot   *by bus: not practical*
🚗: park at the picnic site; the rough road is motorable in a standard car *in dry weather*. Or park in Neo Chorio and walk (50min each way).
A well-sited picnic area, with water, tables and benches; several short walk opportunities in the immediate vicinity (see page 99 and map).

18　Landscapes of Cyprus

22 UPPER KREMIOTIS FALLS OR DROUSSEIA ○ (map page 101)

either picnic by car: 20min on foot　　　　　　　　　　*by bus: not practical*
🚗: park at the fee-paid car park for the Kremiotis Waterfalls (Picnic 22a) or behind the hotel in Drousseia (Picnic 22b) — see Walks 22a and b, page 101.
Follow Walk 22a to the shady picnic area with pool at the upper waterfall or Walk 22b to its 25min-point, where a narrow path leads to the giant rocks (little shade, but fantastic views across to the Troodos, Mount Olympos, Polis Bay and the north coast).

23 MILIOU (map page 105) ○

by car: 25min uphill on foot　　　　　　　　　　　　*by bus: not practical*
🚗: park as for Walk 23 (page 103)
Follow the Short walk to the junction at the 25min-point. Sit on rocks near the track junction, with panoramic views. No shade.

25a FISHERMAN'S TRAIL (map pages 108-109, photo pages 110-111)

by car: 2-10min on foot　　　　　　　　　　　　　　*by bus: not practical*
🚗: park at the signposted nature trail (see Short walk, page 108)
Picnic spots abound on this nature trail — at the water's edge (limited shade) or at the hilltop shelter (shade, benches, fine views).

25b A VIEW FOR THE GODS (map pages 108-109, photo of Germasogia Dam on pages 110-111)

by car: 1h04min uphill on foot　　　　　　　　　　*by bus: not accessible*
🚗: park as for Alternative walk 1 on page 103
Follow Walk 25 from the 31min-point to the 4-way junction at the 1h23min-point. Take the track straight ahead, up to a hexagonal shelter. Views in all directions give you a matchless panorama — from Mount Olympos in the north to the Germasogia Dam in the south, Kouklia in the west and the mountains above Larnaka in the east. Benches to sit on, shade.

27 STAVROVOUNI (map and photos on page 117) ○

by car: 5min on foot　　　　　　　　　　　　　　　　*by bus: not practical*
🚗: park just below the monastery.
From the top of this striking pedestal you have a panoramic view of Cyprus. Women are not allowed in the monastery, but views from the car park are equally impressive. Toilets; sometimes a fruit stall.

28 NEAR KITI TOWER (map and nearby photo on page 119) ○

by car: 56min on foot (8min if you drive to the tower)　*by bus: 56min on foot*
🚗 or 🚌 to Kiti
Follow Walk 28 to the 56min-point and pick your spot on this quiet, pebbly beach. Limited shade, lots of salty water!

29 EAST OF AGIA NAPA (map and photos on pages 122-123) ○

by car: 5-40min on foot　　　　　　　　　　　　*by bus: 15-40min on foot*
🚗: park at Agia Napa near the start of Walk 29 (see page 121).
🚌: check Agia Napa region times and routes at a tourist office.
The early stages of Walk 29 offer numerous picnic opportunities, the best sand being at Kermia Beach (no shade). Head straight there by car if you do not wish to walk.

30 AGII SARANTA (map pages 122-123, photo on page 126)

by car: 20min on foot　　　　　　　　　　　　　　　*by bus: not practical*
🚗: park short of the transmitter tower, then walk round to Agii Saranta, as described in Short walk 30 on page 125.
A pleasant location in the shadow of the unusual little church shown on page 120, set on a hill in the quiet agricultural area inland from the lively resort of Agia Napa.

A country code for walkers and motorists

The experienced rambler is used to following a 'country code' on his walks, but the tourist out for a lark can unwittingly cause damage, harm animals and even endanger his own life. Please heed the hints below.

- **Do not light fires**, except in the areas provided at official picnic sites. Never allow children to play with matches or throw cigarette ends away in the forest. If you see a fire in or near a forest, use the nearest telephone to inform the police or Forestry Department.
- **Do not frighten animals**. By making loud noises or trying to touch or photograph them, you may cause them to run in fear and be hurt.
- **Leave all gates just as you found them**. Although animals may not be in evidence, the gates do have a purpose; generally they keep grazing or herded sheep or goats in — or out of — an area.
- **Protect all wild and cultivated plants**. Leave them in place for others to enjoy. Flowers will die before you get them back to your hotel; fruit is obviously someone's livelihood. ***Never walk over cultivated ground.***
- **Take all your litter away with you**.
- **Do not block roads or tracks**. Park where you will not inconvenience anyone or cause danger.
- **Walkers:** *do not take risks!* Don't attempt walks beyond your capacity. Remember that there is very little twilight on Cyprus ... nor are there any officially-organised rescue services. If you were to injure yourself, it might be a very long time before you are found. **Do *not* walk alone**, and *always* tell a responsible person exactly where you are going and what time you plan to return. On any but a very short walk near villages, carry a mobile, whistle, torch, extra woollie, plenty of water, and high-energy food.

Wild boar are a rare sight — even more so than the elusive moufflon.

Touring

Driving on the roads of Cyprus (keep to the left) can be a great pleasure, but it does at times call for the ability to resist impatience. It can also be tiring in the hot sun. So do not aim for long distances. Better to really *enjoy* a shorter run than simply clock up kilometres. Punctuate days out in the car with short walks and relaxing picnics.

My touring notes are brief: they include little history or information that can be gleaned from standard guides or leaflets available free at all tourist centres and pavilions. Instead, I concentrate on the logistics of touring: road conditions, viewpoints, distances, and good places to rest. Most of all, I emphasise possibilities for **walking** and **picnicking** (the symbol *P*, printed in green on the relevant walking map, alerts you to a picnic spot; see pages 14-18). While some of the walk suggestions may not be suitable for a long car tour, you may discover a landscape you would like to explore at leisure another day.

The tours (which include 4WD suggestions — hiring a jeep is highly recommended) radiate from the three main tourist centres: Pafos, Lemesos and Larnaka. Bearing in mind that

VISITING NORTH CYPRUS

Pedestrians, cyclists and motor vehicles have been free to cross the 'green line' since 2003. It is a simple procedure, similar to any normal passport control. But bear in mind that the Republic of Cyprus authorities will count any time you spend in the north of the island towards your 90-day visa-free total. Another point to consider is whether the Turkish have any different Covid rules in place: check this by keying in foreign travel advice for Cyprus at www.gov.uk.

While it's *possible* to take a hire car to the north, most hire companies specifically preclude this or will not insure you. But it's very straightforward to take public transport to Lefkosia, cross the border on foot and hire a car on the other side.

At present there six active crossing checkpoints, shown on the touring map and the plan of Lefkosia with a red rectangle.

In and to the west of Lefkosia (Nicosia; Lefkoşa in Turkish)
Agios Dhometrios (Metahan in Turkish): Located west of the centre, this is the busiest crossing point — used by vehicles, pedestrians, cyclists, and goods hauliers.
Ledra Palace: Closer to the centre and used by cyclists and pedestrians — no motor traffic except diplomatic vehicles.

Touring

Cyprus is the third largest island in the Mediterranean — some 222 kilometres (138 miles) from east to west — do not plan to tour the *entire* island without an overnight stop or two!

The pull-out touring map is designed to be held out opposite the touring notes and contains all the information you will need outside the towns (town plans with exit routes keyed to the touring map are on pages 8 to 13).

Make sure your **car is in good condition**: keep a regular check on tyres, brakes, water, oil and lights. Always carry warm clothing (especially in the mountains, even in summer) in case of delays or breakdowns. Allow plenty of time for **stops**: my times include only short breaks at viewpoints labelled (📷) in the touring notes. **Distances** quoted are *cumulative* kilometres from the starting point. A key to the **symbols** in the notes is on the touring map.

Some hints: All **motorways** (speed limit 100kph) are toll-free. Some **mountain roads** may be closed in winter. The **blood alcohol limit** is 50mg/100ml, lower than in the UK. **Telephones** (in green kiosks) are located in towns and most villages, near post offices, but most bars and cafes will allow you to make a local call if necessary. **WCs** are available in larger centres; others are found in bars and cafes.

All motorists should read the country code on page 19 and respect the environment.

Ledra Street: Right in the centre of old Nicosia; for pedestrians only.
Zohdia (Güzelyurt in Turkish): Well to the west of Lefkosia, south of Morphou; a crossing point for vehicles, pedestrians, and goods.

British Eastern Sovereign Base Area (two crossing points)
Black Knight: At Agios Nikolaos, for vehicles, pedestrians, and goods.
Pergamos: This checkpoint for vehicles, pedestrians and goods is north of Pyla and Pergamos.

There's a superb selection of walks, restaurants and recipes in Walk & Eat North Cyprus (2010) *by Brian and Eileen Anderson. It's out of print and only available from the Sunflower website as a pdf. While some of the restaurants may be closed, the walks should be viable and the recipes still brilliant!*

Car tour 1: WESTERN WAYS

Pafos • Coral Bay • Pegia • Kathikas • Drousseia • Prodhromi • Lakki • Baths of Aphrodite • (4WD options) • Polis • Skoulli • Stroumbi • Pafos

112km/70mi; about 3h30min driving; leave Pafos on the road to the Tomb of the Kings (Exit D)

On route: ⌐ at Smigies (4WD Route A); Picnics (see pages 14-18) 12, 13, 20, 22, (23); also 14 (4WD routes); Walks (11), 12, 13, 15, 19-22, (23); also 14, 16 (4WD routes)

A leisurely full-day tour on good roads which are narrow and twisting in places. If you've hired a jeep for the first time, either of the suggestions on page 24 offers a good introduction to the joys of rough-track driving! Both 4WD routes make shorter circuits than the full car tour — about 80km in each case.

Leave Pafos on the road to the Tomb of the Kings (E701; Exit D), at the junction between Pafos and Kato Pafos. At 10km pass a signposted turning to the right — a 2km-long road to the Mavrokolymbos Dam (*P*13); it's on the route of Walk 13 from Kissonerga. At 11km reach **Coral Bay**★ (▲△✕☞), the popular beach and resort area shown on page 78, where Walk 13 ends. If you need petrol, head about 1km or so towards Agios Georgios, where you will find a station (⛽) on the right — otherwise …

From Coral Bay, head inland on the E709 to **Pegia** (15km ✝✕☞), a large, cheerful, non-touristy village set on a hillside. As you climb beyond it, the views (☞) over the coast become at first appealing and then magnificent as you head for **Kathikas** (24km; *P*12), which means 'perched on a hill'. Walk 12 sets off from the Laona Project Visitors' Centre behind the church here, and if you find it open, there is usually some interesting literature on display. The Laona Project is a laudable attempt to breathe economic life back into some of the old villages of western Cyprus, while retaining their cultural and social identity. Its ultimate aim is that the entire Akamas Peninsula, including its traditional villages, receives the protected status of a national park.

If you drive through Kathikas and cross the main E711 road, you could detour a few kilometres to Pano and Kato Akourdhalia, two adjoining, small Laona villages noted for springtime almond blossom, a herb garden, folk museum, excellent taverna/guest-house, and the 12th-century church of Agia Paraskevi.

But this tour bears left at the main road for a few minutes, then turns left at a signpost through **Pano** and **Kato Arodhes** (29km) and **Inia** (31km). In this last village, a turning right towards 'Polis' leads to the larger village of **Drousseia** (33km ▲✕☞*P*22; Walks 15 and 22b), with splendid views round

Farmer at Akoursos (Alternative walk 12 from Kathikas)

the compass on a clear day. From Drousseia head east to the E711, or cross straight over the road, following a signpost to Kritou Terra — where there is a very pretty walk to a waterfall and picnic site (see Walk 22a on page 101; photos on page 102).

Continuing north on the E711, you come to the coast road (E713) at **Prodhromi**. Turn left here to reach the fishing port and resort area of **Lakki** (47km ✕; photo on page 4). Not far past the harbour, a fairly new development of luxurious blue and white houses, each one different and beautifully landscaped, catches the eye. Some 7km further on is the CTO restaurant at the **Baths of Aphrodite**★ (✿✕☕*P*20), where Walks 19, 20 and both versions of Alternative walk 21 converge.

Returning on the same road, those with 4WD vehicles may choose one of the options described on the next page, via Neo Chorio, but if you are in a normal hire car you should come back through Lakki (61km) and Prodhromi to **Polis** (65km ▲✕☕ℹ), an appealing town of ancient origin, and once centre of a thriving copper mining industry. From here follow the signposted main road (B7) back towards Pafos, with optional short stops and detours.

Drive through **Skoulli** (75km), and about 8km further on a right turn offers a detour to Miliou (▲*P*23), a tiny Laona village noted for traditional weaving, and the start- and endpoint for Walk 23. A few kilometres further on, a similar right turn (on an exceedingly narrow and winding road) leads to the totally abandoned village of Kato Theletra, where the threat of landslips led to mass evacuation some decades ago. It's an atmospheric place to explore (as can been seen in the photos on page 105), but keep to the streets — the crumbling buildings

4WD OPTIONS

See the reverse of the touring map: normal hire cars could follow this stretch of the 4WD tour as well — going even as far as the Smigies picnic site, but will need to return the same way. I also recommend logging on to the **paphoslife.com** website, where you will learn much about the landscape and its villages.

After visiting the Baths of Aphrodite, head back towards Lakki, but make a right turn and drive 3km to the village of **Neo Chorio**, where there is a new reptile exhibition. You may not be fond of these creatures, but it's useful to know what they look like! Drive carefully through the narrow, winding streets, past the church on your right, and emerge at the far side of the village. Beyond some water tanks on the left, the road reverts to track and forks…

Route A is signposted to **Smigies** — a concrete road leading in about 3km to the church of Agios Minas, from where it continues as a track to the well-equipped Smigies picnic site shown on page 17 (🚗P21), where nature trails start and finish (see Walk 21).

Drive past the picnic site (on your right) and head for the T-junction on the skyline. Turn left, then, after about 150m, turn right in the direction of Koudounas (signposted). Keep going for just under 3km to another junction, where you again turn right towards Koudounas. This rough track (and it *is* rough!) winds westward toward the coast road which you reach some 6km beyond the T-junction at Smigies. The views are wonderful.

Turn left and drive about 7km to **Lara Beach** (*P*14; Walk 14; photo on pages 14-15). The track is rutted, but gives access to a number of secluded beaches where you could skinny-dip with impunity, or picnic to your heart's content. From Lara, continue on the unmade road past the signposted Viklari taverna on your left and the turn-off to the Avagas Gorge (Walk 16; photo on pages 80-81). After 6km you come into **Agios Georgios**, now on an asphalted road.

From Agios Georgios, where there is a small harbour, rock tombs and a church of 6th century origin, you have a simple drive of about 20km to **Pafos**, via Coral Bay and Kissonerga.

Route B follows Route A to the fork beyond **Neo Chorio**. Here turn left past a goat enclosure and drive for 5km to the once-Turkish village of **Androlikou**, which was abandoned during the Turkish occupation of the island in 1974 … after which the village was home to a single Cypriot family, a few sheep, a few pigs, a few noisy dogs … and around 1000 goats. There are signs that people are coming back — perhaps some of whom work at the largest quarry on the island, dug below the village in recent years to the horror of environmentalists.

Now head for 'Pittokopos' — on asphalt. Just over 1km along, where the asphalt bends left, you could go straight ahead on an unsigned track to another abandoned Turkish village — **Fasli**. If you keep to the asphalt road, you soon come to a villa development in the middle of nowhere, **Pittokopos**. At a shelter/viewpoint with picnic table about 500m further on, turn sharp right for 1km, then turn left for wonderful views over the coast. This appallingly rutted track takes you to the coast road, just above **Lara Beach**. Your return to **Pafos** is as Route A.

Above: spring on the Agiasma Nature Trail at Kathikas (Walk and Picnic 12); right, from top to bottom: disused spring at Kato Arodhes; poppies and daisies; giant fennel (Ferula communis)

could be unsafe. Old Theletra is the mid-point of Walk 23 — a superb hike.

A huge eucalyptus welcomes you to **Stroumbi** (95km ✗); there used to be some enchanting reliefs along the roadside here; I hope they will be replaced. Some 6km further south, a right turn would take you to the monastery of Agios Neophytos, shown on page 75 (✝📷; Walk 11) — an optional detour of 8km return. From **Mesoyi** (105km), it's a short drive back to the centre of **Pafos** (112km), after a day spent exploring a varied and unhurried region of the island.

Car tour 2: OLD VILLAGES, ROCKS AND BONES!

Pafos • Geroskipou • Kouklia • Pano Arkhimandrita • Dhora • Arsos • Omodhos • Episkopi • Kourion • Petra tou Romiou • Pafos

130km/81mi; about 3h30min driving; Exit A from Pafos
On route: Picnic (see pages 14-18) (18a, 18b); Walks 17, (18)
A full day's tour, packed with variety and interesting scenery — mostly on good asphalted roads (but sometimes on terrible ones!)

Head out of Pafos on the B6 Lemesos road (Exit A; Leophoros Georgiou Griva Dhiyeni). The first village, effectively a suburb of Pafos, is **Geroskipou** (3km ✝♠✕☗M), renowned for *loukoumi*, the delicacy shown opposite. Call it Turkish delight if you wish, but not within Greek earshot. One of only two surviving five-domed Byzantine churches on Cyprus stands here, Agia Paraskevi. (The other, at Peristerona, is visited on Car tour 5; see drawing on page 35). Also of interest is the Folk Art Museum: housed in an 18th-century building, it holds an impressive collection of implements both domestic and agricultural, plus rural apparel.

Pass the airport turn-off at **Timi** and, beyond **Mandria** (☗), turn left to **Kouklia** (16km ⛽✕M), site of the Temple of Aphrodite and Ancient ('Palea') Pafos★. It is likely that old Pafos was destroyed by earthquakes in the 12th century BC, and there is little for the casual visitor to see, but the temple and nearby medieval manor are impressive.

Drive slowly through Kouklia. Then a tortuous road, the F612, takes you to **Pano Arkhimandrita** (30km). Walk 17 (an all-time favourite with 'Landscapers') starts here, and it is worthwhile to pause for a short time to visit the shrine of Agii Pateres (see drawing on page 89) and view the scenery which is spectacular on all sides and brilliantly green in springtime, as can be seen in the photo on pages 88-89.

The road continues through tiny **Mousere** and skirts round **Dhora** (37km), to a junction (43km). Keep right for 'Malia', then go left at the next junction (44km), signposted to **Arsos** (48km), a village noted for its dark red wine. Drive in, if you wish, or just take the 'bypass', eventually reaching a Y-fork signposted right to **Omodhos** (60km ✝✕M). This larger village, too, is famed for the

Unusual sights always catch my eye. This 3m-high upright stone near Pakhna is pierced with a hole. A mystery. But one old Cyprus legend suggested that if a man could not crawl through such a gap, he had cuckold's horns!

Market stalls: loukoumi *(top); fruits and nuts*

quality of its wine, and is well worth exploring. The pedestrianised central area is a touch commercial, but you have to buy your wine, *soujoukko, loukoumi,* lace, postcards, olive oil and terracotta pots somewhere, so why not here? Be sure to wander the narrow streets, too, and observe how exquisitely restored many of the houses are. The central Monastery of Stavros is modern but worth inspecting nevertheless.

On the far (south) side of Omodhos, take the fast road (E601) signposted to Lemesos, passing turn-offs to Pakhna, Agios Amvrosios, Pano Kividhes and Kandou, before hitting the B6 coast road beyond the A6 motorway and turning right to drive through **Episkopi** (83km ✕☕M). This is the centre of the British military presence on Cyprus, one of two Sovereign Base Areas — the other being at Dhekelia, east of Larnaka (Car tour 7).

Just beyond Episkopi is the ancient site of **Kourion**★ (🛈✕📷), one of the most important excavations on the island (open daily). Visit the tourist pavilion and acquire all the information you need to make the most of your visit to Kourion and the nearby **Temple of Apollo**★ (🛈). Then continue east above Pissouri, from where you could make a detour to Alekhtora (***P***18a, 18b), either to picnic or to enjoy a short walk overlooking the Khapotami Gorge (Walk 18).

Our last visit for today is to the famed **Rocks of Aphrodite**★ (103km ✕), shown on the cover. There is a tourist pavilion for your refreshment and enlightenment. It is said that the Goddess of Love was born from the sea foaming against the offshore rocks here (of which **Petra tou Romiou** is one; 'petra' means stone). From the rocks, Aphrodite was carried by a shell to the shore — a story most vividly illustrated in Botticelli's painting, *The Birth of Venus.*

Not far beyond Aphrodite's rocks is the Kouklia turn-off where we started up into the hills earlier in the day. From here it's a straight run back to **Pafos** (130km).

Car tour 3: LAND OF THE MOUFFLON

Pafos • Polemi • Kannaviou • Stavros tis Psokas • Dhodheka Anemi • Cedar Valley • Kykko Monastery • Panagia • Chrysorroyiatissa Monastery • Statos • Pafos

about 150-170km/93-105mi, depending on route; 4-5h driving; Exit B from Pafos
On route: ⌂ at Stavros Forestry Station, Cedar Valley; Picnic (see pages 14-18) 10; Walks 9, 10

*A full day's off-road tour for adventurous, confident drivers and passengers in 4WD vehicles (**do not attempt the tour in a standard hire car!**). Although the tracks have been graded and stabilised, they are narrow (with no protection from steep drops), winding ... and subject to rockfall, so allow plenty of time. Those in standard hire cars can still enjoy much of the tour, by approaching Stavros on asphalt (early birds could follow Option 3 on page 33!) and at the end of the tour taking one of the alternative return routes suggested on page 31. Whichever way you travel, the route is packed with variety and beautiful landscapes.*

Take Exit B from Pafos (Leophoros Evagora Pallikaridis, the B7). Some 13km out of town, turn right on the E703, signposted to **Polemi** (16km ▣), a large grape-packing community, and from here continue to **Kannaviou** (24km ✕).

Somewhat over 3km beyond Kannaviou, after passing the wall of the dam, take the track on the left signposted to 'Agia/Stavros tis Psokas/Kykko'. The track, about 20km long, follows the Ezousa Valley. It will take you a good hour or more to reach **Stavros tis Psokas** (45km ●▲⌂), named after a monastery originally sited here, called Stavros tis Psoras ('Cross of the Measles'; the spring at Stavros reputedly held holy water which cured that illness). The forests around Stavros are home to the timid moufflon, but you are more likely to see examples in captivity at the signposted enclosure here at the forest station.

From Stavros continue uphill, observing on the right the start of the Horteri Nature Trail (Walk 9), and come to a junction at **Selladi tou Stavrou** (small signpost). On the left is another short nature trail ('Moutti tou Stavrou', also described in Walk 9). Turn right here towards Kykko and come after about 8km to the **Dhodheka Anemi** junction (another tiny sign; 55km). Park here for a moment and consider walking the 4km to **Mount Tripylos** and back, to break up your day. The views from this peak (1362m/4470ft; **P**10) are magnificent. Walk 10 offers a long, but fairly easy circuit in this area.

The road straight ahead leads to Kykko Monastery after 17km, but it is more scenic to take the signposted road to the right — to **Cedar Valley★** (65km ⌂), a lovely remote basin of tall, majestic cedars. This links up again with the road from Dhodheka Anemi and then comes to a T-junction with the north/south running E912, where you turn right to **Kykko Monastery★** (84km ♦●) — famed throughout the Greek Orthodox world and one of the biggest landowners on Cyprus.

Top and left: Kykko Monastery is almost sumptuous in its decor, compared with more humble retreats. Above: Stavros forestry station, seen — through fog — from the restaurant. Signs point to the moufflon enclosure and to villages and points of interest near and far.

Kykko has an interesting history both ancient and recent; it contains, among other treasures, an icon attributed to St Luke.

Returning from Kykko, turn sharp right just past the tacky tourist kiosks, alongside the monastery wall. Then, at the T-junction, turn right for 'Throni'. The road (F966) winds steeply uphill, past the ornate bell-tower shown overleaf, to **Throni**★ (85.5km 📷), the mountaintop tomb of Archbishop Makarios, from where the views are superb. The archbishop can enjoy them now too: his 10-metre-high, 11 tonne bronze statue, which used to be Lefkosia's main tourist attraction, has been moved here — quite a feat, considering the mountain roads!

From Throni the 4WD tour follows a *very* rough track. Head back through the one-way system at Kykko and turn right when you reach the main E912 road. (See page 31 for the Alternative

return on asphalt roads.) At the next junction (having passed the kiosks again), turn left. Then, at the first left-hand hairpin bend, go straight across towards 'Mylikouri'. Immediately, turn right on a road signposted to the Vryssi Restaurant. After the restaurant the way becomes very rough and narrow — it's the E4 walking route for about the first 16km; then the E4 turns off to the right. Following signage, you eventually come onto surfaced road and the village of **Pano Panagia** (119km), birthplace of Makarios.

Left: bell-tower on the road to Throni.
Below: aerial view focussing on Throni, with Kykko Monastery off to the right.

Car tour 3: Land of the moufflon 31

Beyond Panagia, you have three options for your return to Pafos. You can continue on the good road through Asproyia to Kannaviou, from there retracing the outward journey. But you may wish to see **Chrysorroyiatissa Monastery**★ (🕯♠📷), only 1.5km from Panagia. From the monastery head south to **Statos**, then *either* proceed via Pendalia and the E606 to the coast road and turn right; *or* head for the Pafos–Polis road via Khoulou, Letimbou and Tsadha. Each of the three options brings you back to **Pafos** after about 150km, rounding off a perhaps tiring but spectacular day in high and holy places.

Alternative return on asphalt roads
If you are in a standard hire car, from Throni retrace your route back to **Stavros**. Then take the Lyso road (next to the café and forestry station). This good road winds through thickly forested slopes, with fine views to the mountains and a heady aroma of conifers. Ignore left turns to Sarama and Melandra. Beyond a monument to the EOKA fighters (121km), you come into **Lyso** (124km ✕), a lovely hilltop village with a cultural centre and several tavernas.

Take the road to Polis (F723) on leaving the village, passing **Meladeia** (🍴) before reaching beautifully kept **Peristerona** (126km **M** — not to be confused with the Peristerona near Lefkosia, which is visited on Car tour 5). Together with Lyso, this was a base for the EOKA. It is worth a stop to visit the Byzantine Museum and to view the **Atichoulli Gorge** on the right at the end of the village. Many caves where the fighters lived are visible in the rock face of the gorge, but these cliffs are now the nesting sites of raptors and smaller birds.

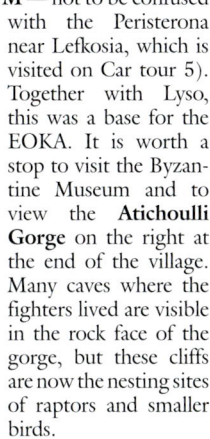

Shortly after leaving Peristerona, look for a sharp left turn, signed 'Pafos' (127km), and follow this road (🍴) above the **Evretou Dam** to the main Polis/Pafos road (B7; 130km). Turn left for the trip back to Pafos (under 160km).

Car tour 4: FROM PAFOS TO PLATRES

Pafos • Asprokremnos Dam • Nikouklia • Phasoula • Agios Georgios • Kithasi • Kedhares • Agios Nikolaos • Pera Pedi • Saittas • Platres

approximately 67km/41mi; about 1h30min driving; Exit A from Pafos

On route: ⌐ around Troodos (see map pages 56-57); Picnics (see pages 14-18) 1-5, 8; Walks 1-6; 8

An easy but pretty drive from Pafos through a picturesque river valley into the Troodos foothills, where you can link up with Car tour 5 if you wish to continue to Lefkosia, and a choice of return routes to Pafos.

It's a lot easier that it once was to reach the Troodos Mountains from Pafos. There is still no *fast* way of doing it, but who wants one?

This is arguably the most direct route, and it is certainly a most attractive morning's drive. Leave Pafos at Exit A on the Lemesos road (B6), and take the second major left turn after the airport turn-off, signposted to (among others) 'Troodos'. You cross the wall of the **Asprokremnos Dam**, which is reached at about 14km. This is one of the larger (and newer) reservoirs on the island. Turn left on the far side to **Nikouklia**.

You are on the F616 in the beautiful Dhiarizos Valley, gloriously green in spring, when the river flows along nicely to your right (later in the year it may be bone dry). On the far side of the river is the abandoned Turkish village of Souskiou, with its old mosque, while a wind farm dominates the skyline.

Car tour 4: From Pafos to Platres

Beyond **Phasoula** (25km), with another poignant disused mosque next to a newish church, proceed very easily through **Agios Georgios**, **Kithasi** and **Kedhares** to **Agios Nikolaos** (44km �ี) which offers a choice of tavernas and some lovely views westward over the upper valley.

After leaving Agios Nikolaos, the road narrows and you start to get impressive views of the Troodos Mountains. Continue to **Mandria**, then turn right on the E802 to **Pera Pedi** (56km; *P* 8 and Walk 8) and **Saittas** (✖). You meet the B8 just before the centre of this latter village, where you should turn left to **Platres★** (67km ▲✖☎🅿⊕). This mountain resort, with its pine-fresh air, has all the facilities you could want, and nearby are many walk options (*P* 1-5; Walks 1-6; see area map pages on 56-57 and photos on pages 51-63).

You can now follow Car tour 5 for a run of about 80km via Troodos to Lefkosia on good roads. But there are several appealing options for a return drive to Pafos.

Option 1: Follow the early section of Car tour 5 in reverse  from Platres to Lemesos (about 40km), then it's another 72km along the coast road back to Pafos.

Option 2: Retrace your route as far as Mandria, then follow signs to Omodhos, from where you can drive part of Car tour 2 in reverse — via Mallia, Dhora, and Pano Arkhimandrita. When you reach the coast road at Kouklia, return to Pafos (about 130km in total).

Option 3: For a really full day, set off early from Pafos to Platres and Troodos, then drive via Prodhromos and Pedhoulas to Kykko Monastery and Stavros. To finish, follow the asphalt road return for Car tour 3 back to Pafos (see notes at the foot of page 31), making a splendid 'Grand Tour' of around 150km covering the west of the island.

Left: in the Dhiarizos Valley; above: the illuminated towers of Pedhoulas church (Option 3)

Car tour 5: A CAPITAL CIRCUIT

Lemesos • Trimiklini • Platres • Troodos • Kakopetria • Galata • Peristerona • Lefkosia • (Stavrovouni Monastery) • Lemesos

approximately 200km/125 mi; about 4-5h driving; Exit A from Lemesos

On route: ⌓ at Platania and Passia's Meadow (both north of Troodos towards Kakopetria on the west side of the road), also Kornos Forestry Station a few miles from Stavrovouni; Picnics (see pages 14-18) 1-5, (7, 8, 25a, 25b, 27); Walks 1-6, (7, 8, 24, 25, 27). (Walk 26 is also best reached from Lemesos.)

A long circuit with many optional detours. Quite easy to accomplish in one day if you like driving, but impossible if you want to do a lot of exploring. It makes an excellent two-day outing with an overnight stay in Lefkosia. All roads are asphalted.

Driving in Lemesos is not for the faint-hearted! The town's traffic management leaves much to be desired, and one should especially be wary of kamikaze moped riders. But here is an escape from such urban perils. Leave the bustling environs of Lemesos at Exit A (the junction of Leonidou I and Makarios Avenue) and follow the 'Troodos' sign. This road (the B8) allows comparatively swift transit from the coast to the mountains in barely an hour. Pass the Polemidia Dam on your left after a few kilometres, then the Kouris Dam, before reaching **Trimiklini** (30km ✕).

After Trimiklini, continue through **Saittas** (✕; easy access to Walk 8 and *P*8) and **Moniatis** before coming into **Platres**★ (37km ▲✕☐☺⊕). This resort is fragmented around the pine-clad hillsides at an invigorating altitude of 1100m/3600ft. Park awhile, and at least explore the central area where you will find shops, banks and a tourist information office. You may also care to look at the Forest Park Hotel, where Daphne Du Maurier wrote the novel *Rebecca*.

You might turn to pages 56-57 before resuming your journey. It is obvious from this 1:50,000 scale map of the Troodos region that Platres is an excellent centre for walkers (especially those with a hire car), and there are many hotels in the area, of all categories. Walk 3 finishes in the centre near the tourist information office; Walk 6 is a short drive away.

From Platres the tour continues up to the trout farm (**Psilon Dhendron**; *P*3, *P*5; Walks 3, 5) and **Troodos** (45km ▲✕☺). Do stop at the Forestry Department's Visitors' Centre on the left (opening hours on page 50), in order to make the most of the area. Troodos is a short way southeast of Mount Olympos★ (👁☺*P*1), the highest point on Cyprus (1952m/6400ft) and focal point for the island's short skiing season from January to March. Unfortunately, it's not worth driving to the summit — it's closed to visitors on account of its military radar installation and TV masts.

The church at Asinou, the finest Byzantine church on Cyprus, is open daily all year round and is a popular tourist attraction, particularly for Russian Orthodox visitors. Murals cover the interior.

Cyprus has hundreds of churches, ranging from tiny bare chapels in remote villages to ornately-decorated edifices containing priceless artefacts. You are likely to come upon long-ruined Byzantine churches with ages-old wall and ceiling paintings still visible. Many an old building is used by shepherds for shelter... for themselves or for their sheep and goats!

It is an unusual village that does not have a church of some kind. If the church is closed, and you would like to see inside it, ask at the local café, where they will readily raise the priest or caretaker, who will open the church for you. If you are exploring a place of worship, remember to dress in suitable clothing. It is also useful to carry a torch for the inspection of dark interiors.

Not every church is distinctive, but that of St Barnabas (Agii Varnava) at Peristerona, shown below, certainly is. Its five-domed structure dates back to the 10th century, and there is only one other five-domed church on Cyprus — at Geroskipou (Car tour 2).

There are mosques in Greek Cyprus, too, but almost all have remained closed since 1974 (a notable exception being Hala Sultan Tekke in Larnaka: see Car tour 6 and photo overleaf).

Walk 1 is a lovely way of experiencing Mount Olympos, although too long for a car touring day. But Walk 2 from Troodos is an easy leg-stretcher, with splendid views to the northeast (**P**2) and the route we are about to cover. The road sweeps past the now-defunct Pano Amiandos mine on the right and the roads to Saittas (🚇 200m from the turn-off) and Kyperounda (**P**7; Walk 7). You pass two official picnic sites to the left (🍴; **P**4; Walk 4) and one to the right (🍴) before coming into **Kakopetria** (60km 🛏🏔✕🚇 and 🛏 Agios Nikolaos 3km southwest) and **Galata** (64km 🛏🏔✕) — foothill villages which both reward exploration if you have the time, especially if you enjoy old churches.

This route (B9) goes straight to Peristerona, but consider first a 28km return detour to Asinou church★ (see panel on page 35) from the Koutraphas crossroads, via Nikitari. Beyond **Peristerona** (85km 🛏), head straight for **Lefkosia**★ (117km 🛏☕🏔✕🚇⊕🛈M), the attractions, sights and peculiarities of which are fully detailed in tourist office material. If you are staying overnight, you might consider a brief crossing (on foot) into North Cyprus at the Ledra checkpoint (see pages 20-21), and you should certainly see the colourful Laiti Yitonia area near the city centre, the Venetian walls, the Cyprus Museum, and the ancient Cathedral of St John.

Leaving Lefkosia on Archbishop Makarios Avenue (Exit A on the town plan on pages 8-9), reach the A1 for a swift return to Lemesos in an hour or so. But a detour of about 18km return to Stavrovouni Monastery★ (**P**27 and Walk 27; Car tour 6; photo on page 117) is highly recommended. Other possible excursions off this route include the lace-making centre of Lefkara, but this could prove costly, as the good people of Lefkara will do their utmost to persuade you to spend! You may care to dally at Governor's Beach, still popular with British expats and where there is a pleasant beachside café, or call at Agios Georgios Alamanou. Walk 24 starts at this distinctive blue and white monastery, shown on page 107. Beyond here you pass the road to Kellaki (photo on page 109), from where Walk 25 descends to the Germasogia Dam (shown on pages 110-111; **P**25a) just northeast of **Lemesos**, which you should reach after some 200km, *without detours*.

Right: flamingoes at Hala Sultan Tekke's Salt Lake (Car tour 6)

Car tour 6: THE HEIGHT OF ORTHODOXY

Larnaka • Hala Sultan Tekke • Kiti • Dhromolaxia • Kalok-horio • Pyrga • Stavrovouni Monastery • Kophinou • Larnaka

approximately 100km/62mi; about 3h driving; Exit B from Larnaka

On route: ⌒ at the Kornos Forestry Station a few miles from Stavrovouni; Picnic (see pages 14-18) 27, 28; Walks 27, 28

*A full day out from Larnaka, taking in a Moslem holy place, one of the finest churches on Cyprus and the pinnacle of Stavrovouni. All roads are asphalted. **Note**: Women are not allowed to enter Stavrovouni, nor is photography permitted.*

Take the B4 road south to the airport (Exit B) for the start of this compact tour, and notice the shimmering whiteness of the Salt Lake, which is exploited commercially in the summer

months. In winter, if it rains and the lake fills up, it becomes a refuge for thousands of flamingoes and other migratory birds.

Just past the airport, turn right to palm-shrouded **Hala Sultan Tekke**★ (5km ☼⛫✕), the third most important place of Moslem pilgrimage, after Mecca and Medina. It is a shrine revered as the burial place of the prophet Mohammed's aunt. Take off your shoes and go inside...

'Twas in the mid-7th century during an Arab raid on the island that Umm Haram, maternal aunt of the prophet, was travelling with her husband when she fell from her mule and broke her neck. She was buried at once 'in that fragrant spot'. The location, shown on page 37, is indeed beautiful, with the mosque and its minaret surrounded by gardens and trees. It is as much frequented by tourists as pilgrims these days, and there is a restaurant nearby. Excavations to the west of the mosque have revealed the site of a Bronze Age town and many historically valuable artefacts.

After visiting the Tekke ... put your shoes on again and return to the main road, turning right to reach **Kiti** village (11km ☼✕), which is notable only for the church shown on page 120 — the magnificent Panagia Angeloktistos★ ('built by angels'). It houses the finest Byzantine mosaics on Cyprus. Walk 28, which takes in a Venetian watchtower and another lovely church (photos on page 119) starts and ends nearby. If you've packed bathing things, you might like to try a short version of this hike (*P*28).

Come back on the same road as far as **Meneou**, then turn left (signposted) to pass through **Dhromolaxia**, shortly reaching a crossroads, at which keep ahead to **Kalokhorio** (26km ☼). Head for **Agia Anna**, then turn left for **Pyrga** (35km ☼✕).

Some 1.5km beyond Pyrga you will meet the old B1 (Lefkosia/Lemesos road); there is a petrol station just to the right. This is the best access to the Kornos Forestry Station picnic site (⌇), south of here, off the A1. Turn left and after another 1.5km find the signposted turn-off left to Stavrovouni. The monastery is reached after an unprepossessing drive of 10km — past a quarry and an army camp (remember not to take photographs in this area). **Stavrovouni Monastery**★ (48km ☼☞*P*27) is the goal of Walk 27. The approach is by way of a series of hairpin bends, but the road (once a rough track) is now asphalted. The views are astounding.

After your visit, follow the *old* Lemesos road south as far as **Kophinou** (70km ✕), and then turn left for a straight run back to **Larnaka** (about 100km).

Car tour 7: THE FAR EAST

Larnaka • Dhekelia crossroads • Phrenaros • Dherinia • Paralimni • Protaras • Cape Greco • Agia Napa • Xylophagou • Larnaka

100km/62mi; about 3h driving; Exit A from Larnaka
On route: ⊼ at Xylotimbou; Picnics (see pages 14-18) 29, 30; Walks 29, 30
A full day, offering a variety of popular beaches, quiet seaside picnic spots, country roads ... and a view to Famagusta in North Cyprus. All roads are asphalted; a few are narrow.

Hit the B3 Dhekelia road north out of Larnaka (Makarios III; Exit A), first passing a light industrial area, with petroleum storage tanks much in evidence. But having left these behind, you are heading for the southeastern extremity of the island, which boasts the best beaches and accompanying crowds, but has a quiet charm, too. A wide variety of produce is grown in the rich red soil. Water is a precious commodity at the agricultural end of the island, and windmills abound, drawing water out of the ground to irrigate crops of potatoes and other vegetables.

As the industrial area ends, the beaches start, and to your right you will see a shoreline which is recreational for several

The modern church of Profitis Ilias at Protaras is most attractive. Many lovely old churches can be explored in this area — among them the little cave church of Agii Saranta, shown on page 126 (Picnic 30). Both Profitis Ilias and Agii Saranta are visited on Walk 30.

kilometres, offering watersports, hotels, apartments and restaurants.

At the **Dhekelia crossroads** (14km) head north on the E303, following signposting for Famagusta. You pass a turn-off for Pergamos (crossing point for North Cyprus; see pages 20-21). The road bends around Xylotimbou (🅿) and then Athna in North Cyprus. Our route passes through a corridor of the British Eastern Sovereign Base Area, leading almost to Agios Nikolaos (where there is another crossing point).

Turn right short of 'Aye Nick' (as the locals call it) and head along the E329 to **Phrenaros** (38km) and from there take the E305 to **Dherinia** (42km ✕), only a few kilometres from Famagusta in North Cyprus. In the opposite direction (our continuing route) lies the larger village of **Paralimni** (45km ▲✕🍴). Follow the signs for Protaras and Cape Greco for a few kilometres, almost on the coast, passing through an area noted for its forest of windpumps — a vital part of the irrigation system in this agricultural region.

At **Protaras**★ (57km ✝▲✕) there is an excellent beach and ancillary development which mushroomed in the early 1980s. Be sure not to miss the lovely church of Profitis Ilias (shown on the previous page) while you're here. The whole area between Protaras (or 'Fig Tree Bay', as it is also called) and Agia Napa is splendid for picnicking and walking. Those of you who want a real constitutional

The hot Cyprus sun can do strange things to one's body. Here at Nissi Beach, as afternoon shadows lengthen, these sunseekers are oblivious to the way they look after hours of trying to achieve a golden-brown, all-over tan. Very easy to do at Nissi, but don't stay too long. Meanwhile, the fellow at the top obviously has a touch of sunstroke. He thinks he has scored with a beach beauty. But don't squeeze too hard, friend, or the lady will go to pieces...

Car tour 7: The far east 41

can combine Walks 29 and 30. For suggestions, a large-scale map, and more photographs of this area, see pages 121 to 126.

The road continues south, turns sharp right above Cape Greco and the Radio Monte Carlo transmitter masts, and continues to **Agia Napa**★ (66km ✝▲✕🚻⊕*P*29, *P*30), another much-developed tourist area, thanks to its fine beaches. At the centre of Agia Napa is an again-thriving monastery, used now as an ecumenical centre. Note the 600-year-old sycamore at its entrance.

The return to Larnaka passes the turn-off to Nissi Beach, heading then (partly on the A3 motorway) via **Xylophagou** (78km ✕), a market-gardening centre, and **Dhekelia** (86km) back to **Larnaka** (100km).

Walking

In this Ninth edition of the first-ever walkers' guide to Cyprus, I describe routes covering about 400 kilometres (250 miles) of the best rambling on the island. The walks are designed to show you as painlessly as possible the wide variety of Cyprus landscape and to take you through a few communities not often troubled by the tourist trade. In these villages, you will find the island at its most heartwarming. The welcome will be genuine and hospitality generous to those who rest awhile.

Do consider combining some walks. We've indicated where routes overlap on the walking and touring maps. But *never try to get from one walk to another on uncharted terrain!* Only link up walks by following paths described in these notes or by using roads or tracks; don't try to cross rough country (which might be dangerous) or private land (where you might not have the right of way).

There are walks in this book for everyone.

Beginners: Start on the walks graded ● or ●, and check all the short and alternative walks — *and the picnics!*

Experienced walkers: All the walks in the book should be within your stride, even the occasional scrambling.

Bus users and motorists: Wherever possible, we have tried to cater for you. The long linear routes usually have shorter circuits for motorists as an alternative.

All walkers: Please follow the routes as described in the notes, and if you are at any stage uncertain of the way forward, go back to the last 'sure' point and think again. Do **not** try to continue a walk where bulldozers or natural damage such as a landslide — even on a well-maintained nature trail — has made the way impassable or dangerous.

Grading, waymarking, maps, GPS

Each walk's **grade** is shown in the Contents, but see the walk itself for full details. Here is a brief overview:

● very easy — more or less level (perhaps with a short climb to a viewpoint); good surfaces underfoot; easily followed

● easy-moderate — ascents/descents of no more than about 300-500m/1000-1800ft; good surfaces underfoot; easily followed

● moderate-strenuous — ascents/descents may be over 500m/1800ft; variable surfaces underfoot

● difficult — only suitable for very experienced hillwalkers

Walking 43

Any of the above grades may be followed by:
! *danger* of vertigo — you must be sure-footed and agile, with a very good head for heights

The authorities on Cyprus have gone to great lengths to **signpost** and **waymark** some nature trails (99 at last count!). If you log on to www.visitcyprus.com (the official website for southern Cyprus) and search 'nature trails' there is a list of most of them, with an interactive map which shows where they start. There is also a brief description of the various trails, but no walk *directions*. Unfortunately waymarking is often lacking at junctions. Some of the trails are quite tough, others (such as Walk 12) may be subject to landslides and potentially hazardous.

For all the routes described in this book, the accompanying

Goats on the Akamas uplands, in mist

maps should suffice. Originally prepared with reference to maps published in 1960s/70s by the Department of Lands and Surveys in Lefkosia and the British Ministry of Defence, they have been greatly updated with reference to Google Earth and GPS readings taken on the ground. A good **printed map** of the Troodos area is usually available free from the tourist office in Platres. Other printed maps *may* be available on the island, but web searches usually end up linking to Google Maps.

Free **GPS track** downloads are available for all the walks in this book: see the Cyprus page on the Sunflower website. Please bear in mind, however, that GPS readings should *never* be relied upon as your sole reference point, as conditions can change overnight.

Where to stay

For purely a walking holiday on Cyprus, an obvious area to head for is the mountainous **Troodos region**. Its focal point is Mount Olympos, and within a 25km radius you have a wide choice of walking opportunities. I have described the more accessible routes. Platres, a hill resort with shops, restaurants, banks, hotels and apartments, is the most popular centre, but there are others — Troodos, Prodhromos, Pedhoulas and Kakopetria among them.

At **www.visitcyprus.com** there is a searchable database of places to stay. It covers accommodation from five-star luxury hotels to economical self-catering apartments.

There is **good coastal walking**, plus splendid beaches, around the Agia Napa/Protaras area on the southeastern corner of the island. To the southwest there is pleasant strolling around Pafos. Interesting walking excursions can be made from Larnaka (notably to Stavrovouni, but also out to the southeast). If you're based at Lemesos, the Troodos region is reached in under an hour by road.

But increasingly, walking enthusiasts are enjoying the **Akamas Peninsula** in the northwest corner of the island, an hour or less from Pafos. You will need your own transport to do this area justice, and I would recommend hiring a 4WD vehicle. The hills, valleys, gorges and wild coastline around places like Polis, Lakki, Drousseia, Kathikas and Lara are still completely unspoiled, with some excellent possibilities for rural accommodation.

Basic facilities may be available at some (but not all) of the island's **monasteries**, but bedding is *not* provided. No charge is made, but a donation on departure is appreciated. This privilege is really intended for Greek Orthodox pilgrims, and as a tourist, if you really want somewhere cheap to stay, it is more appropriate to seek out a room in a village. This is a great help to the fragile rural economy, and you will get a good deal and a cheap, authentic Cypriot meal.

Accommodation for a maximum of three nights is available at the **Stavros Forestry Station** (see page 69), where there is also a campsite; book in advance (tel 26-991858).

A highly satisfying way of exploring Cyprus on foot for the first time would be to **combine a week in the Troodos with a week on the coast**. That way, you would have time for some of that sun, sand and brandy sour!

Weather

The Cyprus climate is splendidly Mediterranean, with constant sunshine during much of the year, and with rainfall being confined to a fairly short and predictable winter, when temperatures remain at a pleasurable level.

The walker probably experiences Cyprus at its climatic best between March and early summer, when the countryside is a blaze of floral colour and the sun hot, but not unbearably so. September and October are good walking months too.

The high Troodos region is cold in winter (and can be so beyond Easter), with snow usually allowing skiing for about eight weeks on the slopes of Mount Olympos. Summer temperatures here can be high, but they are usually a few refreshing degrees cooler than on the coast and consistently cooler than in Lefkosia, where the mercury can go above 38°C (100°F) for days on end!

Important: Anyone planning a walking trip early in the year should note that rainfall can turn dry tracts into streams and rivers. Moreover, there might still be snow in the mountains, making trail-finding impossible.

AVERAGE TEMPERATURES

Month	Average air temperature Min °C	°F	Max °C	°F	Average sea temperature °C	°F	%age of days with sun
Jan	8.9	47.9	18.3	65	16.5	61.4	57
Feb	9.4	49	19.4	66.9	16.9	62.4	63
Mar	10	50	20.6	69.1	17.3	63.2	67
Apr	12.2	53.9	22.8	73.1	18.6	65.5	71
May	15.6	60.1	27.2	81	21.1	69.9	79
Jun	18.3	65	30	85.9	24	75.3	87
Jul	22.8	73.1	35.6	96	26	79.4	90
Aug	22.8	73.1	35.6	96	27.8	81.9	88
Sep	18.3	65	32.2	90	27.6	80	88
Oct	17.2	63	27.8	82	25.1	77	80
Nov	12.2	53.9	23.9	75	21.9	71.4	71
Dec	8.3	46.9	17.2	66	18.9	66.4	59

What to take

If you are already on Cyprus when you find this book and do not have items like a rucksack or walking boots, you can still enjoy a number of the easier walks, or you can buy some equipment in one of the sports shops. Please do not attempt the longer or more difficult walks without the proper equipment. For each walk described, the absolute minimum gear is given. Do adjust the equipment according to the season; for instance, take a long-sleeved shirt and long trousers, as well as a sunhat, in summer months, and a fleece and rainwear on cooler days.

Where walking boots are prescribed, there is, unfortunately, no substitute. You will need to rely on their grip and ankle protection and, occasionally, their waterproof qualities. If you do wear shoes, make sure they have rubber soles, preferably of the Vibram or Skywalk variety. The often stony and dusty tracks of Cyprus can be unforgiving toward the improperly shod walker.

Please bear in mind that neither I nor the Sunflower team have done *all* the walks in this book under *all* weather conditions. We may not realise just how hot or how wet a walk can be, depending on the season.

Nevertheless, if you intend going to Cyprus properly kitted out, you may find the following checklist useful. I rely on your good judgment to modify your equipment according to circumstances and the season. It is always wise to seek out local advice about conditions before undertaking any walk, especially in the hills.

- walking boots (which must be broken-in and comfortable)
- waterproof gear (outside summer)
- smartphone (the **emergency number is 112**)
- torch (if only for inspecting the darkened interiors of ruined churches!)
- long-sleeved shirt (sun protection)
- long trousers, tight at the ankles
- trekking pole(s)
- small/medium-sized rucksack
- up-to-date transport timetables
- safety pins, string, clips
- lightweight jacket
- knives and openers
- first aid kit
- rainhat
- groundsheet
- water bottle
- extra pairs of socks
- windcheat (zip opening)
- warm fleece
- sunhat, suncream
- extra bootlaces
- whistle, compass
- telephone numbers of taxi operators

Walkers' checklist

The following cannot be stressed too often:
- **NEVER walk alone** — four is the best walking group.
- **Do not overestimate your energy**. Your speed will be determined by the slowest walker in your group.

Walking 47

- **If a walk becomes unsafe**, do not try to press ahead.
- **Transport connections** at the end of a walk may be very important.
- **Proper shoes** or boots are vital.
- **Always take a sunhat** with you, and in summer a cover-up for your arms and legs as well.
- **Warm clothing** is needed in the mountains, especially in case you are delayed.
- **Mists** can fall suddenly in the mountains.
- **Always carry water and rations** on long walks.
- In spring, normally-dry **riverbeds may be flooded**.
- **Compass, whistle, torch, mobile or smartphone** weigh little, but could save your life.
- **A stout stick** (or trekking pole) is a help on rough terrain and to discourage the rare unfriendly dog.
- **Do not panic** in an emergency.
- **Re-read the important note** on page 2 and the guidelines on grade and equipment for each walk you do.

Nuisances

Thankfully there are few nuisances to worry about when walking on Cyprus, but goat enclosures are often guarded by noisy **dogs**. If dogs worry you, you might like to invest in a 'Dog Dazer' — an ultrasonic dog deterrent, which persuades aggressive dogs to back off without harming the dogs. These devices are available on the web at reasonable prices.

It should be noted that poisonous **snakes** are indigenous to the island, along with non-venomous varieties (see page 6 under 'Books': *Nature of Cyprus*). The chances of an encounter are slim, as snakes are shy creatures. As a precaution, however, it is wise to check under rocks or logs (perhaps with your walking stick) before settling down for a picnic, especially if you are somewhere very hot, close to water. Examples of Cyprus reptiles, including snakes, are on view at the Herpetological Society's new snake park at Neo Chorio on the Akamas Peninsula. Neo Chorio is one of the options for 4WD with Car tour 1, but it is easily visited in a standard hire car — see page 24 and the reverse of the touring map.

Lizards of all shapes and sizes abound, but these are good fun!

Photography

Photography is forbidden in some sensitive areas (eg near military bases or the 'green line'), but warning signs make any restrictions clear. Some museums and churches do not allow photography ... it is good manners to ask, in any case.

Greek for walkers

In the major tourist areas you hardly need to know any Greek at all, but once you are out in the countryside, a few words of the language will be helpful, and people will be grateful for your attempts to communicate.

Here's one way to ask directions in Greek and understand the answers you get! First memorise the few 'key' questions given below. Then, always follow up your key question with a second question demanding a yes ('ne') or no ('ochi') answer. Greeks invariably raise their heads to say 'no', which looks to us like the beginning of a 'yes'!

Following are the two most likely situations in which you may have to use some Greek. The dots (…) show where you will fill in the name of your destination. I'd recommend that you purchase an inexpensive phrase book: many give easily understood pronunciation hints, as well as a selection of phrases.

■ ASKING THE WAY
Key questions

English	Approximate Greek pronunciation
Good day, greetings	**Hair**-i-tay
Hello, hi (informal)	**Yas**-sas (plural); **Yia**-soo (singular)
Please — where is	**Sas** pa-ra-ka-**loh** — **pou ee**-nay
the road that goes to …?	o **thro**-mo stoh …?
the footpath that goes to …?	ee mono-**pati** stoh …?
the bus stop?	ee **sta**-ssis?
Many thanks.	Eff-hah-ree-**stoh** po-**li**.

Secondary question leading to a yes/no answer

Is it	**Ee**-nay
here?/there?/straight ahead?/	e-**tho**?/eh-**kee**?/kat-eff-**thia**?/
behind?/to the right?/	**pee**-so?/thex-**ya**?/
to the left?/above?/below?	aris-teh-**rah**?/eh-**pano**?/**kah**-to?

■ ASKING A TAXI DRIVER TO TAKE YOU/COLLECT YOU

Please —	**Sas** pa-ra-ka-**loh** —
would you take us to …?	Tha **pah**-reh mas stoh … ?
Come and pick us up	**El**-la na mas -reh-teh
from … (place) at … (time)*	apo … stees …*

*Point on your watch to the time you wish to be collected

Organisation of the walks

Each ramble in this book was chosen for its accessibility from one or more of the main tourist centres on Cyprus. Walks 1-8 are ideal for anyone staying in the **Troodos/Platres** area. Walks 9-10 are accessible too, but are set in mountainous country, remote from any major centres, and a considerable journey is necessary to reach them, wherever you are based. From **Pafos**, Walks 11-13 are nearest, but if you have a car consider too Walks 9 and 10, 17 and 18, and *all* walks west of the Polis road (B7). From **Polis and Lakki**, Walks 15 and 19-23 are close at hand, but Walks 9 and 10 and all routes north of Pafos are easily reached by car. **Lemesos** is the recommended base for Walks 24-26, but Walks 1-8 and 17 and 18 are within reasonable driving distance. Walks 27 (Stavrovouni Monastery) and 28 are best approached from **Larnaka**, but Walk 27 is worth some kind of excursion from *wherever* you are staying! Walks 29 and 30 in the **Agia Napa** region are also accessible from Larnaka.

I hope the book is set out so you can plan your walks easily. You might begin by considering the fold-out map inside the back cover. Here you can see at a glance the overall terrain, the road network, and the location of all the walks. Flipping through the book, you will also find at least one photograph for each walk. Having selected a potential excursion from the map and the photographs, look over the planning information at the beginning of the walk. Here you'll find distance/hours, grade, equipment, and how to get there and return (by public and private transport). Wherever feasible, I have also suggested a short version of the walk, for those lacking in time and/or ability.

When you are on the walk, you will find that the text begins with a brief introduction and then quickly turns to a detailed description of the route itself. The **large-scale maps** (all 1:50,000) have been annotated to show key landmarks and waypoints. Times are given for reaching certain points on the walk. Giving times is always tricky, because they depend on so many factors, but the times I give are rather slower than my own walking time. **Note that they do not include any stops**! *Allow ample time for stops — you may need to even double these point-to-point times!*

Below is a summary of the symbols used on the maps:

motorway	spring, tank, etc	specified building
trunk/other main road	church.chapel	transmitter mast
secondary/minor road	shrine or cross	cave.windmill
loose-surface road	cemetery	quarry, mine.mill
jeep track	picnic tables	watchtower.stadium
path, trail	best views	fire-watch tower
main walk	bus stop.parking	forestry house
alternative walk	walk start/waypoint	ancient site
other CTO trail	CTO signpost	picnic suggestion (see pages 14-18)
E4 long-distance trail	military warning sign	map continuation
height (50 m intervals)	castle, fort	

Walk 1: ROUNDING MOUNT OLYMPOS

See map pages 56-57; see also photos on pages 1 and 61
Distance: 13.4km/8.3mi; 4h
Grade: ● quite easy; gentle ups and downs between 1700m and 1750m, with an eventual height gain of 100m/330ft up to the Artemis Trail
Equipment: walking boots or stout shoes, fleece, sunhat, water, picnic; waterproof in winter
Transport: 🚗 to/from Troodos; park at the northern end of the main street, at the junction with the E910, opposite the Post Office (34° 55.416'N, 32° 52.852'E). Or park at the Visitors' Centre southwest of the main square (34° 55.300'N, 32° 52.648'E) and start there. Or 🚌 to/from Troodos (Timetables A7, A9 and B7). *Note:* The Visitors' Centre is usually open daily from 10.00 until 15.00 (16.00 in summer), but is closed on Christmas Day, New Year's Day and Easter Sunday.
Shorter walk: Troodos to Chromion (9.5km/6mi; 2h30min; ● easy). Follow the main walk to Chromion (**6**); arrange to be collected there.
Alternative walk: Artemis Trail (7km/4.3mi; 2h; ● quite easy, with gentle ups and downs between 1800m and 1850m). 🚗 to the start of the nature trail, some 0.4km up the road to the Olympos summit (34° 55.993'N, 32° 52.331'E). Or access the trail by following the main walk and joining Artemis at **2**.

There is a riding stable at Troodos, so the description of 'one horse town' is not entirely accurate. It nearly fits, but development has seen a Forestry Department Visitors' Centre replacing the open-air kebab houses with their squabbling owners. I miss them! Still, Troodos is neither a town nor a village, but a collection of shops, small hotels, cafés and souvenir stalls. It's a community that springs to life at weekends and in summer and is the centre of activity during Cyprus's short ski season. Four kilometres from Troodos by road is the highest point on the island — the summit of Mount Olympos (1952m/6400ft). Though romantically named, it is the site of a TV transmitter and radar base (the latter featuring an enormous landmark 'golf ball') and is closed to visitors. Still, this circuit remains one of my favourites in the Troodos.

Start the walk at the stone-built POST OFFICE at the northern end of the main B9 road in **Troodos** (**O**; just south of the junction with the E910). Follow the path behind the building, in 100m/yds coming to an INFORMATION BOARD for the **Atalante Nature Trail** (**1**). The path curves round the back of the JUBILEE HOTEL (**8min**), much favoured by skiers and walkers, then doubles back on itself at the head of a small 'gulch', which is a dry as a bone most of the year. Keep left at a FORK (**2**; the right option links to the Artemis Trail and is our return route). As the trail contours at about 1750m, soon you can look south towards Platres and beyond. At about **25min** a wide panorama opens up, with even the Salt Lake at Lemesos visible on a clear day.

When you reach an open area with picnic potential and

Walk 1: Rounding Mount Olympos 51

striking views (❸; **45min**; Picnic 1), ignore the wide track up to the right and follow the GREEN HIKERS' SIGN as the trail passes a wooden bench. Ten minutes later (**55min**) observe a stream of drinking water on the right (but it may be dry in summer). Continue along the trail, admiring the wonderful views to the

Troodos in snow — very pretty, but make sure you don't try to follow any of the trails if the powder is still deep!

south, until you arrive at the tunnel entrance to the HADJI-PAVLOU CHROMIUM MINE (**4**; **1h25min**), which was worked during the 1950s. Keep out, if you have any sense! But you'll find shade here for a refreshment stop. A couple of minutes later follow the TRAIL SIGN to the left.

At a VIEWPOINT (**5**; **1h50min**) observe to your left Prodhromos village and the distinctive, abandoned (and reputedly haunted!) Berengaria Hotel. On the horizon you'll see Throni, the peak above Kykko Monastery where Archbishop Makarios is buried. The trail becomes a little scree-like for a short way (**2h05min**). A few minutes later, notice a small abandoned QUARRY to the right, and soon look up for a clear view of the Mount Olympos TV mast.

A stone building below on the road signals **Chromion**, the end of the nature trail (**6**; **2h30min**; *not signposted*). Exit here the weary, the sun-struck and the tight of schedule. Onward the rest of us! Walk to the back of the stone building and then head diagonally uphill for around 100m/yds (two-three minutes) to reach the very clearly visible **Artemis Trail** (**7**), where you turn left. The trail crosses TWO SKI RUNS and gains a little height. At the second ski lift, walk between the stone building and behind the building housing its mechanism to find a HIKERS' SIGN and continue on your trail. Soon after the second lift there are some striking views across to North Cyprus and west to the coast above Pafos.

At **3h** you should reach the secondary road leading to the TOP OF **Mount Olympos**, opposite the INFORMATION BOARD marking the START OF THE ARTEMIS TRAIL (**8**; Alternative walk). I don't think it's worthwhile trudging up asphalt just to say I've been to the top, but if you choose this detour, allow 3km/1h return. The Artemis Trail is another, slightly shorter (7km) circuit of Mount Olympos, not vastly different from the one just completed, but higher and a touch more dramatic. Save it for another day *or* combine both trails for a good long ramble.

For the main walk, start out along Artemis then, when the trail crosses a wide track between two METAL TRAIL INDICATORS (**9**) after seven or eight minutes, leave the trail and turn sharp left downhill on a track through pines. (Or shorten the walk by keeping ahead for 25 minutes back to Troodos.) Seven or eight minutes later (**3h15min**) turn left on a rocky track which descends gently as it curves around the hillside and 20 minutes later rejoins the Atalante Trail. Turn left again, back to **Troodos** (**0**; **4h**), after a splendid introduction to Mount Olympos. Views are spectacular all year round, with richly coloured flora in spring, and you will have barely climbed a hill all day.

Walk 2: MAKRYA KONTARKA

See map pages 56-57; see also photos on pages 1 and 61
Distance: 6.7km/4.2mi; 1h55min
Grade: ● easy, with under 100m/330ft ascent/descent overall
Equipment: trainers, sunhat, water, picnic; fleece/waterproof in winter
Transport: as Walk 1, page 50

Alternative walk: Troodos — Kaledonia Falls — Platres (12km/7.4mi; 3h40min; ● fairly easy descent of 600m/1970ft). At the crossroads in 35min (❶), turn right and follow an easy, rough forestry road (E4) for about 5km to **Kryos Potamos** (info board), where you can pick up Walk 3. Or link up with Walk 5; there are endless permutations!

This splendid, easy stroll packs a wide variety of scenery into a short distance. It's a lovely way of getting some Troodos air after a drive up from the coast.

Start at the ROUNDABOUT (◯) at the southern end of **Troodos**, where a minor road rises to the signposted POLICE STATION. Follow the road or the crazy-paving path below it up to the POLICE STATION, opposite which you fork left on the signposted **Persephone Nature Trail**.

In about **15min** you come to this attractive stand of tall pines; these benches have long since been replaced (Picnic 2). You don't need a rest yet, so keep going until you reach an obvious VIEWPOINT (**23min**), from where you can look back the way you have come and enjoy a fine view of Mount Olympos. Then look ahead: to the left you'll see the unmistakable landmark of the (closed) Pano Amiandos asbestos mine, with the road to Kakopetria, Galata and Lefkosia just to its left. If you travel that road during your stay, you will get an different view of the mine from the other side — it was a mighty excavation!

Take note of a '2KM' sign on the right and keep straight ahead, following the regular trail signs. You walk between two LOW STONE WALLS (**40min**), followed by a long series of stone steps leading down towards a crossroads with a trail board (❶). Go straight across and follow the trail past a '3KM' sign to **Makrya Kontarka** (1680m/5510ft; ❷; **55min**; Picnic 2). There are plenty of seats — an ideal place to settle down with a flask and sandwiches to enjoy breathtaking views of Pano Amiandos, Trimiklini and Saittas villages, the peaks of Kionia and Kakomallis ... not to mention Lemesos harbour and Salt Lake, plus countless village vineyards.

Return to **Troodos** the same way (**1h55min**) or, if you prefer a circular walk, go back to the junction with the trail board and turn right: follow the dirt road around the valley to just below the POLICE STATION (**1h50min**).

Walk 3: TROODOS • KALEDONIA FALLS • PLATRES

See map pages 56-57; see main photo opposite and other photos on pages 1 and 61

Distance: 6km/3.7mi; 2h05min

Grade: ● quite easy descent of about 600m/1970ft, *but beware of turned ankles* where the stony path (which can be slippery) twists and turns.

Equipment: stout shoes or walking boots, sunhat, water, picnic; fleece and waterproof in winter. In spring, be prepared to get your feet wet!

Transport: as Walk 1, page 50 (by 🚗, park at the Visitors' Centre in Troodos). For the return, take a taxi from Platres back to Troodos for your car, or 🚌 (Timetables A7, B7)

Alternative walks
1) Begin on 'Persephone' (Alternative walk on page 53);
2) See the map: climb back to Troodos with Walk 5 if you're fit!

At the entrance to Psilon Dhendron — if you've not taken a picnic, you might like to stop for a trout lunch before heading on to Platres.

The Kaledonia Nature Trail itself is a mere 2km long. But the going requires some attention because of twists and turns in the path and stepping stones which criss-cross the stream many times on your way to the falls.

Start out at the VISITORS' CENTRE west of the main square in **Troodos**: from the CAR PARK (○), walk just a few paces left on the main road, then turn right down the quiet old zigzagging B8 road (not signposted at time of writing).

After about 2km (**30min**) you come to a wooden CTO 'KALEDONIA NATURE TRAIL' ARCHWAY (❶) below the PRESIDENT'S SUMMER COTTAGE. Take the path under the arch. Now stop and listen ... for if it's high summer you may be hearing your first babbling brook of the holiday. Many streams dry up in summer, but not the **Kryos Potamos** ('Cold River').

There are numerous stream crossings, and *take care* on the steep wooden or stone steps, especially in wet weather. Nimble walkers might reach the **Kaledonia Falls** (❷; Picnic 3) in **1h05min**. But those of us peering at all the points of interest on the nature trail — and the less fleet of foot — might take around **1h15min**. Stay on the downhill path below the falls, following the stream. Half an hour later, the aroma of grilled trout heralds the TROUT FARM and restaurant (**Psilon Dhendron**; ❸; **1h45min**). Cross the road and continue into **Platres** (❹; **2h05min**).

Left: The Kaledonia Falls

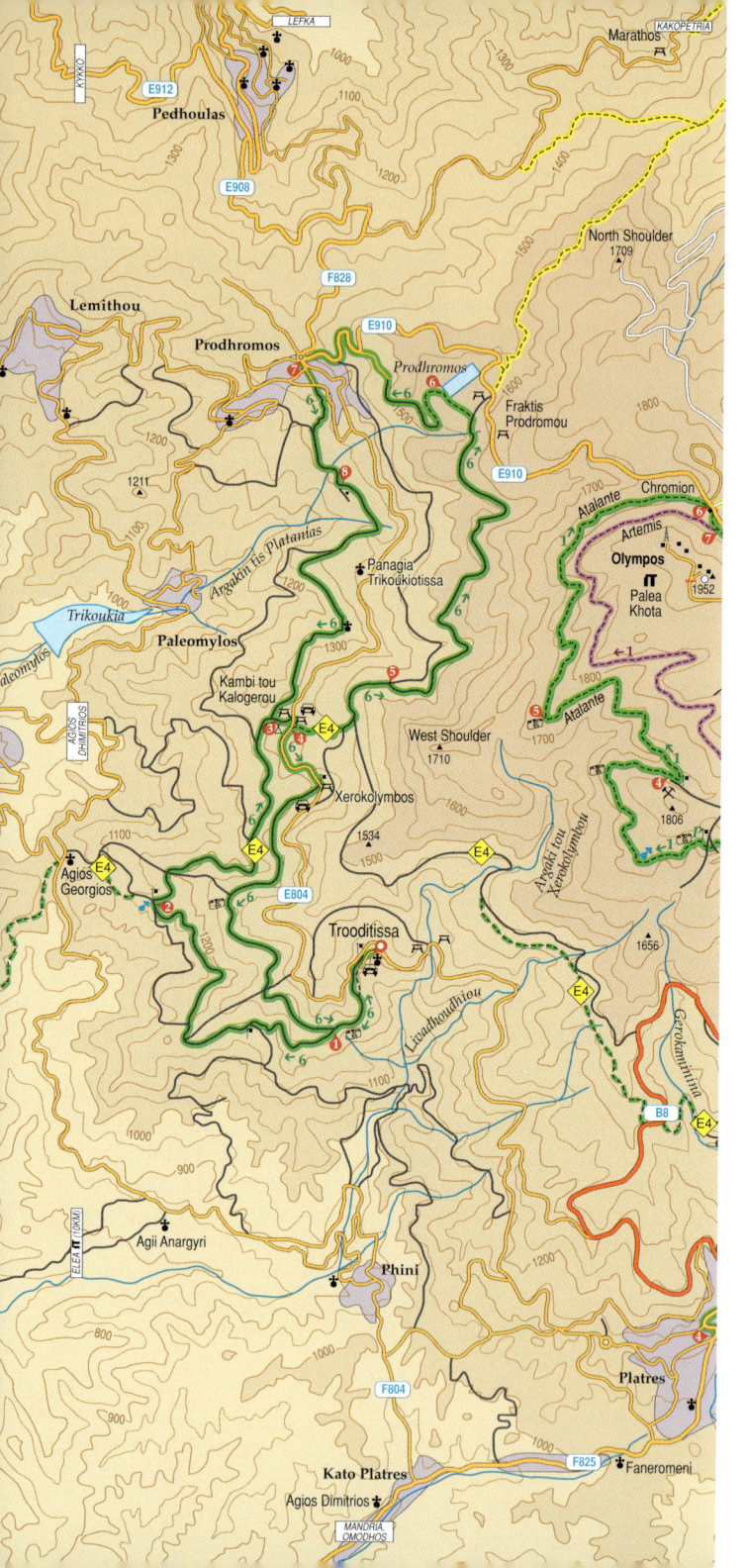

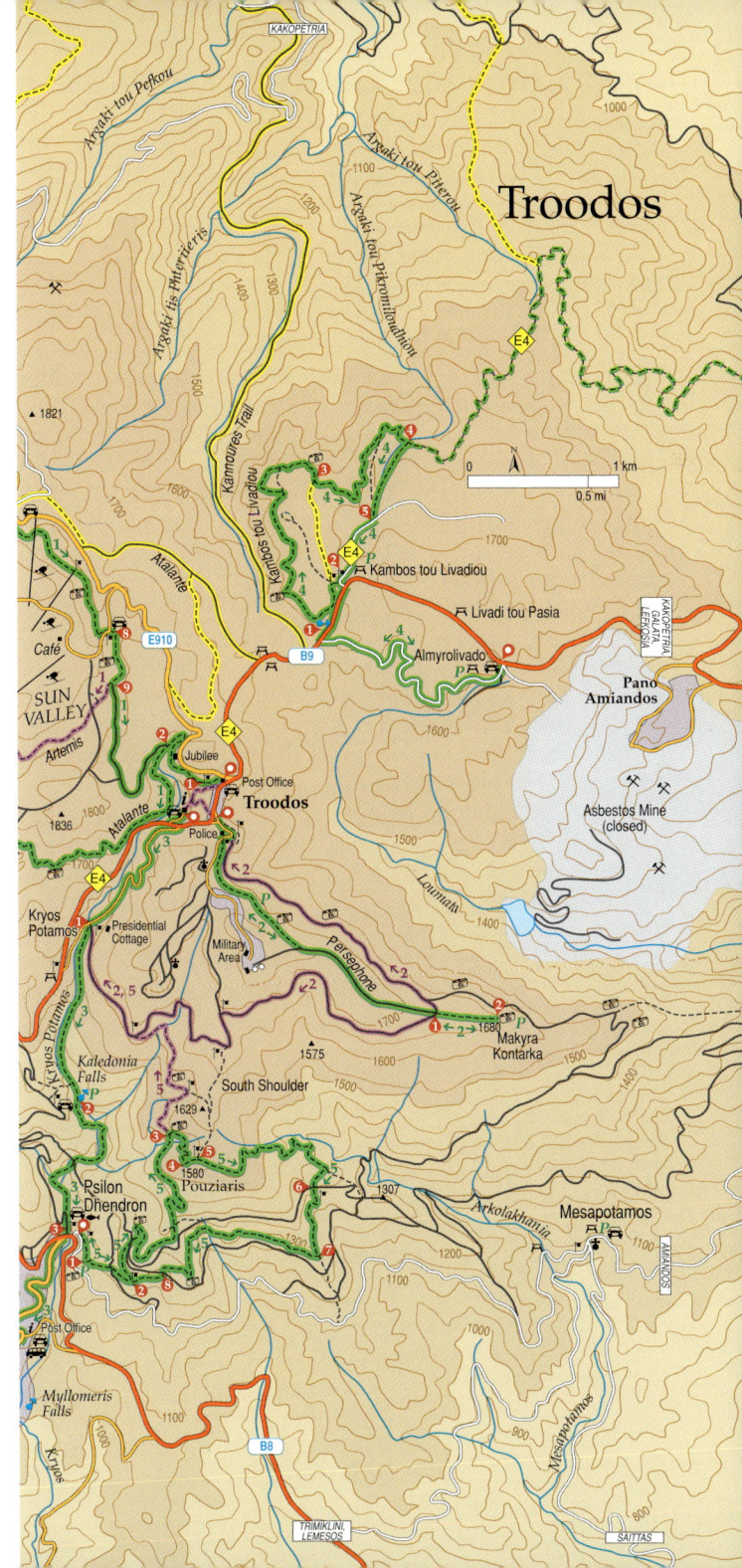

Walk 4: ALMYROLIVADO AND KAMBOS TOU LIVADIOU

See map pages 56-57; see also photos on pages 1 and 51
Distance: 9.8km/6mi; 2h35min
Grade: ● quite easy walking at altitude on clearly defined roads and tracks with only moderate changes in gradient (ascent/descent of about 150m/490ft overall). Plenty of shade throughout.
Equipment: stout shoes, water, picnic; fleece and waterproof in winter
Transport: 🚗 to the the Almyrolivado picnic site (34° 55.851'N, 32° 54.184'E). From Troodos Square, take the B9 road towards Lefkosia for around 2.5km, to this picnic site on your right

This is a very pretty route high up in the Troodos Mountains. You will walk in the shadow of Mount Olympos and enjoy some spectacular views across forested hillsides into steep ravines and to the north coast, all without any real exertion!

Start the walk at the **Almyrolivado picnic site** (⓿): look for the old green road sign (set back from the site) which points toward Troodos and set off along this disused road, ignoring a track off left almost at once. On your left is some precious peat grassland, a rare habitat on the island. As you walk along this quiet old road, there are some good views early on across to the white 'golf balls' marking the Troodos summit. Look out for Bonelli's Eagles soaring high above you and imagine the days (not so long ago) when this narrow, winding — and occasionally precipitous — route was the only way to approach Troodos from Lefkosia. How times change!

When the old road rejoins the B9 (**30min**), turn right, passing a SPRING (❶) on your left after just over 100m/yds. A short way further on is the **Kambos tou Livadiou** picnic site with nature trails (**35min**). Turn left into the site and walk a few metres up the asphalt road until you see TWO SIGNPOSTS (❷), one pointing left to Trails 1 and 2, the other straight on along the road to Trail 3. For the most part we'll follow TRAIL 2, so turn

The split pine at the 1h10min-point

Walk 4: Almyrolivado and Kambos tou Livadiou 59

left here, into the pines. You immediately reach an INFO BOARD on the left marking the official start of both trails; at 1650m/5400ft, you are not far below the island's high point of 1952m.

You pass strategically placed benches and a couple of wooden structures housing toilet facilities as the path initially winds around the southwestern contours of the mountain. After a few minutes you emerge from the pines — to a clear view of Mount Olympos to your left with the deep river valley plunging below you. As you continue along the marked trail, you'll pass the thick trunk of a PINE TREE (**1h10min**), still thriving but cleft in two by a lightning strike — a dramatic foreground to more views of Mount Olympos.

The path winds round to the northern side of the mountain, briefly passing an impressively steep drop falling away to your left before reaching a signposted VIEWPOINT with a wooden bench (**1h20min**). Rest here awhile, to enjoy the breathtaking views down the valley to the spa town of Kakopetria and across to Morfou Bay and the Mediterranean in the north.

When you are ready to carry on, follow the track behind the bench to a junction with arrows and signs. With the viewpoint behind you, turn left and continue eastwards along TRAIL 2 (❸) as it contours around the mountainside. In a minute or two you will see a signpost indicating 'MNIMATA PISKOPON' (Piskopon footpath) and Kakopetria. This is your route.

You will head north, then east, through quiet, mixed pine forest where young cedars have been planted among the black pines to help with reforestation. Ignore a track to the right (**1h31min**). A few metres further on an E4 SIGN on a tree, followed by a wooden bench in a large clearing confirms your route. Continue following E4 markers.

Come to a T-JUNCTION (❹; **1h43min**): A LARGE SIGN FOR THE E4 long distance path points left to Kakopetria and right to Troodos. Turn right to join the main E4 back towards Troodos. Follow this signed forest track through the trees until it emerges on a LANE, still the E4 (❺; **1h51min**). Turn right here (don't go left — this is a restricted military area!) and walk briefly down the asphalt road. After about 10 minutes you will find yourself back at the TWO SIGNPOSTS for the Kambos tou Livadiou nature trails (❷; **1h59min**).

From here just retrace your steps, crossing the B9 road and heading downhill for a few minutes before turning left and walking back along the old Troodos–Lefkosia road. You should arrive back at the **Almyrolivado picnic site** in around **2h35min**. If you haven't yet had your picnic, you can head downhill for a few metres, to where there are plenty of benches and tables in the trees overlooking the grasslands.

Walk 5: POUZIARIS NATURE TRAIL

See map pages 56-57; see also photos on pages 1, 51, 54 and 55
Distance: 8.2km/5mi; 2h40min
Grade: ● moderate, with an ascent/descent of 400m/1300ft; good paths throughout
Equipment: stout shoes, sunhat, water, picnic; fleece and waterproof in winter. In spring, be prepared to get your feet wet!
Transport: 🚗 to the car park for the Pouziaris Nature Trail at Psilon Dhendron (30m east of the car park for the Kaledonia Falls; 34° 53.749'N, 32° 52.112'E), both just off the main B8 road. Or 🚌 to Platres (Timetables A7, B7) and walk to Psilon Dhendron

Alternative walk: Psilon Dhendron — Kryos Potamos — Kaledonia Falls — Psilon Dhendron (10km/6.2mi; 2h55min; ● moderate, with an ascent/descent of about 400m/1300ft, sometimes on stony paths; access and equipment as main walk). Follow the main walk to the 50min-point (❸). Take the path straight ahead and reach the rough forest road linking the Persephone Trail to the Kaledonia Falls Trail (1h05min). Turn left and, from the **Kryos Potamos** shelter (1h20min), follow Walk 3 back to **Psilon Dhendron** (2h55min).

This is a wonderful circuit, with plenty to interest the nature lover and some marvellous views from the highest point. The ascent route follows an ancient mule trail, and the lovely woodland paths are full of bird life.

Start out by climbing the path to the left of the POUZIARIS NATURE TRAIL BOARD (O; just off the start of the signposted track to Mesapotamos). The path winds right and rises steadily through shady pines and junipers. As you bend left, notice the bench off to the right at a VIEWPOINT (❶; **6min**, Picnic 5) and a few strawberry trees, providing food for birds rather than for you! You'll see many more of them later in the walk. Cross a forestry road, going slightly left (**11min**). Five minutes later, turn left at a junction (❷; **16min**) and follow the route marked 'TROODOS SQUARE 8KM'. (The path to the right is your return route). Now on a wide old MULE TRAIL, you enjoy magnificent views back over Lemesos and Platres.

Cross another forest road (**22min**), again going slightly left to follow the path uphill and eventually reach a welcome bench overlooking the Kryos Valley (**40min**). Round the slopes, with steep drops to the left, cross the bed of a stream (often dry) and after just 25m/yds turn right uphill on a path indicated by a sign fixed to a tree (❸; **50min**). *(But for the Alternative walk take the path straight ahead.)*

The woodland path rises to the SUMMIT of **Pouziaris** (❹; **1h03min**) — not really a peak, just a plateau marked by a wooden signboard. After taking in the superb views over the south coast from the bench here, continue a few steps to a junction (❺; **1h05min**): Troodos is signposted as 6km, but you should head downhill, following the sign for 'PSILON DHENDRON 6.5KM'. Your path now zigzags downhill with a few steep and stony sections. Descending through pines interspersed with more strawberry trees, you pass a bench (**1h35min**).

Ten minutes later you cross a FORESTRY ROAD (**6**; **1h45min**). Carry straight on along the signposted path — a rocky downhill stretch, followed by another SHARP TURN TO THE RIGHT (**7**) and a long steady ascent. A large rockfall is easily negotiated and eventually you reach another welcome bench with views across the trees (**2h15min**). The path then winds to the right and descends quite sharply, to meet a forestry road at the foot of a few steps (**8**; **2h23min**).

Cross this track, heading slightly right, and pick up your onward path. Continue down to the old MULE TRAIL coming in from the right (**2**; **2h26min**). Having rejoined your outward route, you'll soon hear the welcome sound of running water at the trout farm and come to **Psilon Dhendron** (**O**; **2h40min**).

Above: the strawberry tree (Arbutus unedo) *features prominently on this walk.*
Below: when it snows in the Troodos, everyone heads for the mountains.

Walk 6: TROODITISSA

See map pages 56-57; see also photo on page 1
Distance: 20.6km/12.8mi; 5h25min
Grade: ● moderate, but long, with a sustained ascent of 550m/1800ft; good earthen roads underfoot; plenty of shade
Equipment: walking boots or stout shoes, sunhat, water, picnic; fleece and waterproof in winter
Transport: 🚗 to Trooditissa, on the E804 northwest of Platres. Park in the car park just outside the monastery gates (34° 54.776'N, 32° 50.298'E). Or 🚌 to Platres (Timetables A7, B7), then taxi to start and return.

Shorter walk 1: Kambi tou Kaloyerou circuit from Trooditissa (10km/6.2mi; 2h55min; ● easy, with one ascent of 175m/575ft; access as main walk). Follow the main walk to ❸ (1h40min), then pick up the notes again at the 4h10min-point to return to Trooditissa.

Shorter walk 2: Prodhromos circuit from Kambi tou Kaloyerou (10.6km/ 6.6mi; 2h30min; ● moderate (ascent of 360m/1180ft); 🚗 to the picnic site (E804 north of Trooditissa; 34° 55.654'N, 32° 49.915'E). Join the walk at ❸ (1h40min) and follow it back to ❸ (the 4h10min-point).

Trooditissa Monastery, nestling in the Troodos Mountains some 5km northwest of Platres, was founded in 1250, and among its treasures are ancient icons and a leather belt decorated with silver medallions. Tradition has it that wearing the belt promotes fertility in women. Until a couple of decades ago, one of the monks would happily produce this potent object for visitors, but perhaps because of increasing tourism, a large sign now proclaims that the monastery is not open to tourists — although if you are suitably attired you will have no problem visiting. In any case, this a very scenic walk, with endless permutations, only two of which are our suggested short walks.

Start at **Trooditissa** (○): walk through the wooden gates, with the monastery to your left and emerge on a clear dirt track. You pass a bench and shelter (**7min**) and as the route curves round to the southwest, you enjoy magnificent views over Phini village in the valley far below. When you reach another track leading off to the right (❶; **20min**), ignore it for the moment — it's the return route. Continue down to the left, to a signpost indicating 'PHINI 4KM' (**25min**). Ignore this too!

At a clearing with a ROUND WATER TANK (❷; **50min**) a signpost indicates Agios Dhimitrios straight ahead, but we turn right ('PRODHROMOS 5KM'), for a gentle climb of 2.5km. You are now on the E4 long distance path, with early views of Prodhromos nestling in the hills up to your left and the famous Berengaria Hotel on the skyline above. At a fork (**1h30min**), ignore the sign to Palaiomylos left; go right and continue uphill to the **Kambi tou Kaloyerou** CAMP- and PICNIC SITE (❸; **1h40min**) on the E804 road.

After taking a break in this pleasant location, cross the E804

Entrance to Trooditissa, rock roses and cress

and walk 50m/yds to the right downhill, rejoining the E4 trail signposted at the left of the road (**4**). Rise up this track, passing to the right of a CONCRETE WATER TANK, until you reach a T-junction with a wide dirt track. Turn left here, *leaving* the E4 route which heads off to the right. A minute or two later, ignore the sign pointing right to Asprokremmos; keep ahead for 'PRODHROMOS DAM 4KM'. After another seven-eight minutes, go right at a fork (**5**; **2h**). Keep along this track as it continues to climb steadily through scented pine forest and, at a signboard, turn left to the PICNIC SITE at the **Prodhromos Dam** (**6**; **2h40min**).

After taking a break, follow the crazy-paving path towards the toilets. But leave it for a rocky downhill trail to the left, just in front of wooden railings. Meeting a clear dirt track next to some telegraph poles, turn left and follow it in a U-turn *away* from Prodhromos at first. But at a T-junction with another track, turn sharp right, back towards the village. This

becomes a concrete road, passes some houses, then joins the Prodhromos/Troodos road (E910). Turn left, passing a fine hillside viewpoint with shelter.

At a ROUNDABOUT (**7**) at the entrance to **Prodhromos**, walk down the narrow cobbled street behind the minimarket (a YELLOW PILLAR BOX is on the left). Cross a road and carry straight on along the steep concrete/cobblestone road, passing a house with green shutters on the right, then water tanks with goldfish, vineyards and orchards. Ignore tracks left and right; then, at a Y-FORK WITH A SMALL HUT straight ahead (**8**; **3h25min**), take the path to the left. You pass a deep fissure on the left after 500m/yds and after another 500m/yds you can fork left uphill (**3h40min**), back up to **Kambi tou Kalogerou** (**3**; **4h10min**).

Now head south on the E804 for about 10 minutes, then turn right on a track signed 'TROODITISSA 3KM' (**4h20min**). Follow this gently downhill, back to your outward route (**1**; **5h**). Turn left, retracing your steps back up to **Trooditissa** (**0**; **5h25min**).

Walk 7: MADHARI RIDGE

Distance: 7.5km/4.7mi, 2h30min; optional extra 3.5km (1h) round Mount Adelphi

Grade: ● moderate climb of under 300m/980ft; some short, steep stretches

Equipment: walking boots or stout shoes, sunhat, water, picnic; fleece and waterproof in winter

Transport: 🚗 by car, leave Troodos on the Lefkosia road (B9). Beyond Pano Amiandos, turn off right for Kyperounda. After about 4km, turn left towards 'Spilia 5km'. Park 1.8km along, at Doxasi o Theos, where there is an information board on the right (34° 57.358'N, 32° 57.776'E).

Alternative walks: Two other CTO nature trails are highlighted on the map below *in yellow*. GPS are available for both from the Sunflower website. A much-loved circuit ● leads from **Doxasi o Theos** (◯; where the main walk begins) north to **Moutti tis Choras** (❺), then east along the E4 to **Selladi tou Karamanli** (❻), south to **Adelphi** (❹) and then down along the **Madhari Ridge** back to **Doxasi o Theos** (◯). Total distance 13km/8mi; about 4h30min-5h, with climbs/descents of about 500m/1640ft overall. The other trail ● follows the E4 between two charming Byzantine churches — **Stavros tou Agiasmati** (❼; a detour off the Peristerona road) and **Panagia tou Araka** (❽) near Lagoudhera. This out-and-back walk is 15km/9.3mi; 5h, with ascents of 600m/2000ft. To halve the distance/ascent, leave your car in Lagoudhera and call a taxi from one of the coffee houses, to take you to Stavros tou Agiasmati. Walk from there back to your car.

Mount Adelphi is the second highest point on Cyprus (1613m/5290ft), and this walk to it along an exposed ridge is even more spectacular than the approach to Mount Olympos. It can be strenuous for short stretches, and the track

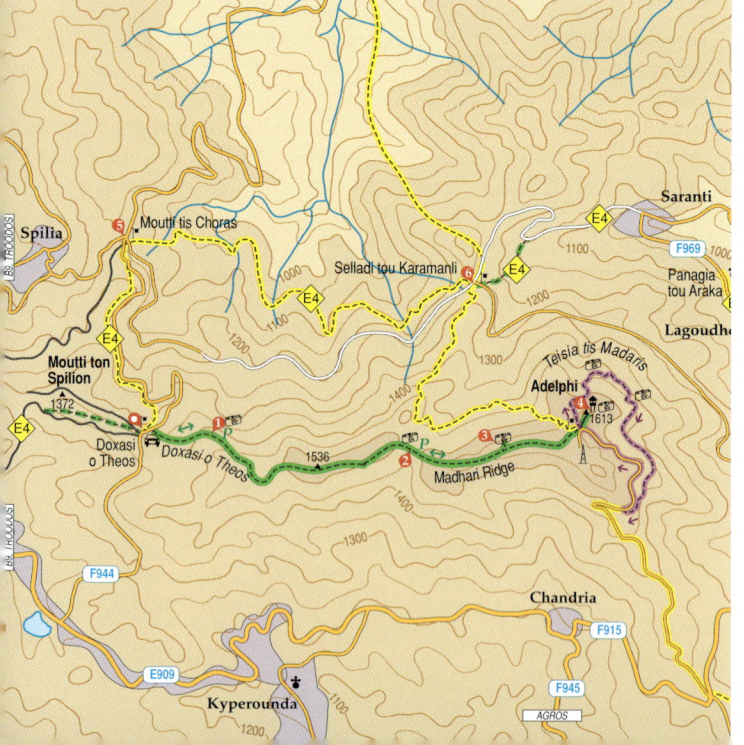

Walk 7: Madhari Ridge 65

stony, but the views are stunning — from the northern, Turkish side of the island, to the south, where Kyperounda clings to the opposite hillside like magic.

Start out at the INFORMATION BOARD for the **Doxasi o Theos** ('Glory to God') **Nature Trail** (**○**): follow the wooden sign 'MADHARI 3.75KM' as the path zigzags uphill through the pines. You soon reach a rocky outcrop with a wonderful view north towards Morphou Bay. At around **15min**

The highly decorated Byzantine church of Panagia tou Araka — on the E4 trail near Lagoudhera (one of the Alternative walks)

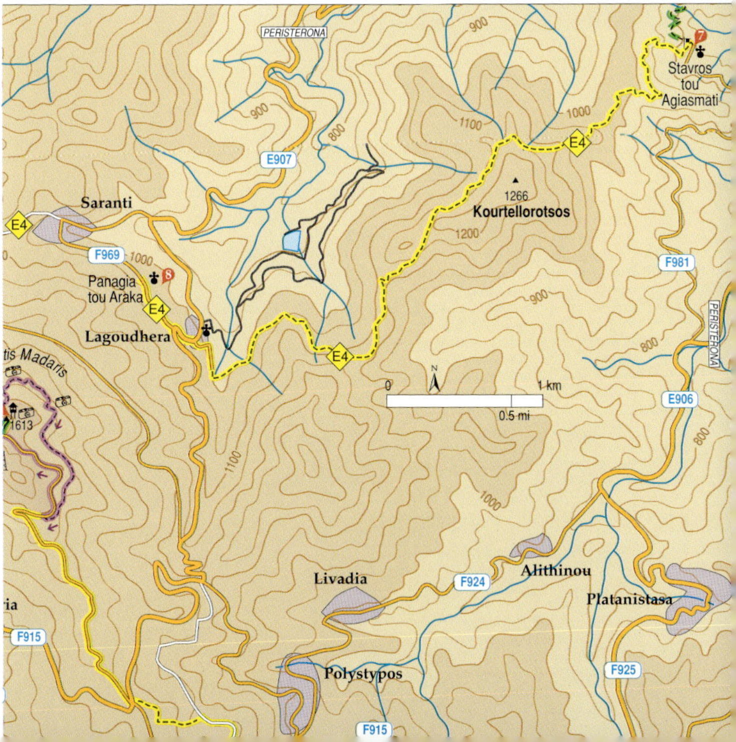

come to one of several well-placed benches (❶; Picnic 7) from where there are equally breathtaking views over Kyperounda and towards the abandoned Pano Amiandos asbestos mine and the Olympos 'golf ball'.

Walk the trail through pine trees, then drop down to a SMALL CLEARING with views through a more recent plantation over the Mesaoria Plain and towards Mount Adelphi — another setting for Picnic 7 (❷; **40min**). This could mark the end of a short version of this walk if you didn't fancy the climb ahead. But it isn't as bad as it looks, honestly! It can be quite cool and breezy on top, even in summer.

Skip up to the TOP OF **Madhari Ridge** (**50min**) like a moufflon, and you'll be rewarded with wonderful views! You'll see Kyperounda again to your right, and Chandria with its striking modern church. Reservoirs glimmer between the two villages. White cairns indicate VIEWPOINTS to your left (❸; you climb slightly to reach them), then the FIREWATCH POINT at the peak comes into view. From the CTO board below the peak, climb the last stretch to the SUMMIT OF **Mount Adelphi** (❹; **1h20min**) for some truly magnificent views — and, if you wish, do the extra signposted 'Teisia tis Madaris' circuit (add *at least* one hour to do this).

Then retrace your steps to the **Doxasi o Theos** INFORMATION BOARD (O; **2h 30min**). If you haven't been impressed by the views from the ridge, the brandy sours are on me if we ever meet!

Mount Adelphi and the fire-watch station

Walk 8: CIRCUIT FROM PERA PEDI

Distance: 11.3km/7mi; 2h40min
Grade: ● fairly easy, with an ascent/descent of about 300m/1000ft; all on country roads and lanes; *very little shade*
Equipment: stout shoes or trainers, sunhat, water, optional picnic
Transport: 🚗 to Pera Pedi (the 56km-point in Car tour 4). Park in the car park (34° 51.749'N, 32° 52.377'E) and walk on to the Neromylos Village Inn on the main street. Or 🚌 to Platres (Timetables A7, B7) and taxi

Short walk: Agia Mavri (6.7km/4.2mi; 1h40min; access, equipment, ● grade as above (ascent/descent about 180m/600ft). Follow the main walk to ❷ (1h), then turn left to the E802 and left again, back to the start.

Alternative walk: Extension to Lofou (17.3km/10.7mi; 4h40min; access/equipment as above; ● moderate but long (ascents/descents of about 400m/1300ft). Follow the main walk to ❷ (1h), then turn right at the crossroads. Entering **Lofou**, make your way to the main church (❺). With your back to its blue gates, walk down a cobbled alley to the left of a lamppost. After about 100m turn left at a hiking sign for 'Y VRISI' Nature Trail (❻). At the end of the trail, head northeast to **Silikou** (❸) and rejoin the main walk at the 1h25min-point, then follow it to the end.

The five villages visited on this walk are very different, and all are delightful. Their livelihood comes from the vineyards you pass en route and, if you have time, you can visit a wine museum and sample the produce in a local taverna. Although the walk follows country roads all the way, they are usually very quiet. (But bear in mind that they are busier at weekends when the town dwellers head out to the villages to visit family or tend their vines.)

Start the walk at the NEROMYLOS VILLAGE INN (〇). Opposite, just to the left, is a crazy-paved pedestrian lane. Follow it over a bridge across the permanently running **Kryos River** (**1min**; Picnic 8). Ignore a fork to the right and turn left at the T-junction with a very old CHURCH (**5min**). Follow this lane as it bends down to recross the river and rises to the road to Agia Mavri and Vouni (**10min**), where you turn right. The road runs alongside the river and through the gorge. At the Y-fork just outside **Agia Mavri** (❶; **25min**), you will turn left. But first have a look at this hamlet with its restaurants and little church.

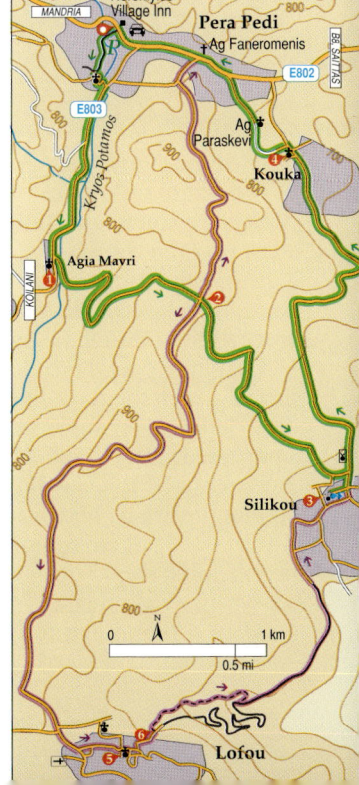

The Laurania Spring at Silikou and vines of the Commandaria wine villages

Back at the Y-fork, now turn right (it should be signposted to SILIKOU). Follow the road in a deep U-bend to the right, then a sharp U-bend to the left. Two kilometres from Agia Mavri, go straight over a crossroads (❷; **1h**). *(The Short walk turns left here; the Alternative walk turns right.)* The road now descends past lovely vineyards to **Silikou** (❸; **1h25min**) — one of the 'Commandaria' wine villages (producing dessert wines for over 1000 years), where there is a small WINE MUSEUM. Next to the village CHURCH you can see the LAURANIA SPRING, set into the trunk of an ancient olive tree.

From Silikou head uphill towards Kouka and Pera Pedi. As you leave the village you will see a rather sadly neglected TURKISH CEMETERY on your left. Continue up to **Kouka** (❹; **2h15min**), another pretty little village. You could pause at a taverna on your left for a pint of real ale from Cyprus' APHRODITE'S ROCK BREWERY. Next door is the church of **Timios Stavros** (Holy Cross). Just a few steps past the church take the left turning which leads uphill. The asphalt road runs out after a couple of minutes and you continue your walk along a loose earth track through some pine woods to the church of **Ag Paraskevi**.

Continue past the church on PARAMBALOU STREET, to the junction with the MAIN E802 ROAD TO PERA PEDI (**2h30min**). Turn left for a couple of minutes, to where a left turn is signposted 'LOFOU 7KM'. Take a look at the SHRINE TO AG FANEROMENIS which is almost opposite this junction. The wax effigies of various body parts here are a rather strange sight to British eyes, but are commonplace in Cyprus' churches, where people leave these votive offerings when they pray for a cure for whatever ails them.

Then continue ahead to **Pera Pedi** (❺; **2h40min**).

Walk 9: STAVROS TIS PSOKAS

Distance: 12.7km/8mi; 4h20min

Grade: ● fairly strenuous: ascents of about 550m/1800ft overall; some gravelly surfaces underfoot

Equipment: stout shoes or walking boots, sunhat, water, picnic; fleece and waterproof in winter; trekking poles for the gravelly descents

Transport: 🚗 by car from Pafos via Kannaviou, then track from the dam (4WD *only*; see Car tour 3 on page 28), otherwise take the E702 via Panagia and Dhodheka Anemi; from Polis via Lyso; from Troodos via Kykko Monastery. Park just over 1km outside Stavros on the Kykko road, by the Horteri Nature Trail information board (on the right; 35° 1.498'N, 32° 38.091'E). Or park at Stavros and start there.

Forestry station at Stavros

Short walks

1 Horteri Nature Trail (5km/3mi, 1h30min; ● moderate-strenuous, with an initial ascent of about 250m/820ft) and a steep descent. Park at the nature trail board and follow the main walk for 1h30min.

2 Moutti tou Stavrou Nature Trail (3km/2mi; 45min; ● easy, with an initial ascent of about 100m/330ft). Park at the Selladi tou Stavrou junction north of the Horteri Trail, by a nature trail information board (35° 1.981'N, 32° 38.103'E). Follow the waymarked trail, going left at a fork (❹), then walking in the *opposite direction* to the main walk (see purple arrows on the map). After 500m, at a junction (🅑), turn right (the path to the left is no longer viable).

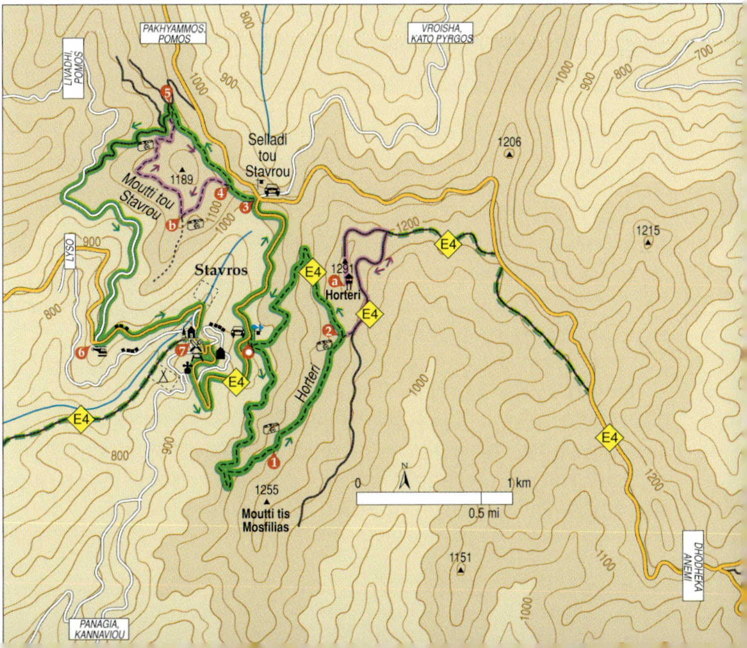

The Forestry Department runs a forest station at Stavros, where there is also a small café and very popular hostel accommodation (see page 45). To encourage intimate acquaintance with the environment, the department has also created

two nearby nature trails, and information about the area is available from the forestry office. Take time, too, to visit the moufflon enclosure just north of the forestry office on the road to Lyso. This rare Cyprus sheep — which was once almost extinct — is a very shy creature, so chances of spotting it in the wild are rare! Since the Stavros nature trails are not adjacent, my 'grand tour' includes stretches of road-walking and could be quite tiring on a warm day. A much easier option is to do the two Short walks as separate circuits.

Begin at the **Horteri Trail** SHELTER/INFORMATION BOARD (by a SPRING; ⭕). Keep ahead at a fork two minutes up (you will return on the path to the left). The path rises gently but steadily through strongly scented pines. Excellent views over the whole valley setting of Stavros and to the fire-watch point

Walk 9: Stavros tis Psokas   71

Chapel of the Holy Cross at Stavros, with Calabrian pine and golden oak

on Horteri are your reward at a first VIEWPOINT (❶). Continue uphill to a fork and benches (❷; **50min**), where you keep left on the nature trail. (Heading right you could climb to the top of Horteri at ❸ for even wider-ranging views over the Akamas Peninsula; allow 45 minutes extra for this diversion.) After a fairly steep descent, the trail descends to the HORTERI TRAIL SHELTER (O; **1h30min**).

From here follow the asphalt road north, to the **Selladi tou Stavrou** junction (❸; **2h10min**). ('Softies' can drive here, to park for Short walk 2.) Climb the steps up to the nature trail and walk ahead to a fork (❹), where you keep right, to *follow the nature trail in reverse* (but for Short walk 2 go *left* here). Soon, from a plateau, there is a fine view reaching west to the Akamas Peninsula. After about 1km you come to a track, where the nature trail path joins sharply from the left (almost back the way you came). *Do not* follow this, but turn sharp left on the *track* (❺). Now just keep heading south on tracks, then the dirt road, keeping left at every junction. From time to time you will enjoy some good views of the Stavros valley.

The dirt road eventually descends to the Lyso road opposite a HELIPAD (❻; **3h30min**), where you turn left to **Stavros** (❼; **3h45min**). From here walk up the Kykko road back to your car at the **Horteri Trail** (O; **4h20min**).

Walk 10: CEDAR VALLEY AND MOUNT TRIPYLOS

See also photo on pages 30-31
Distance: 13.5km/8.4mi, 4h
Grade: ● quite easy, with an ascent of about 330m/1080ft overall; *but note that almost two-thirds of the walk is on road*. If possible, set out early; there may be heavy traffic in Cedar Valley en route to the picnic area or Kykko.
Equipment: stout shoes, sunhat, water, picnic; fleece and waterproof in winter
Transport: 🚗 by car from Troodos via Kykko Monastery, from Pafos via Kannaviou and Pano Panagia, or from from Polis via Lyso and Stavros. Park 8km southeast of Stavros at the junction of the Cedar Valley/Panagia and Kykko roads; there is a road sign here, 'Cedar Valley 8km'. This area is known as Dhodheka Anemi (identified by a tiny brown sign on the Cedar Valley road; 35° 0.581'N, 32° 40.078'E).

Short walk: Mount Tripylos (5km/3mi; 1h40min; access, equipment and ● grade as above, with an overall ascent of 250m/820ft). At Dhodheka Anemi you will see a track (barred to motor vehicles) signposted to 'TRIPYLOS' (if the sign is missing, look for E4 arrows). Just follow this track uphill for 2.5km and return the same way. (Or approach from the Cedar Valley picnic area at ❷.)

Whether you make this walk your prime target for the day, or choose the shorter version while on a trip to Kykko, you are sure to enjoy it! The views are splendid, and the surroundings beautiful. The main (longer) walk will be a disappointment to many, as the loop road into Cedar Valley has been asphalted. But if you'd walked it in the past, swallowing the dust thrown up by 4WD safaris, you'd find it a great improvement … especially out of season or early in the day, when there's little traffic.

Begin at the **Dhodheka Anemi** JUNCTION (❶): follow the road signposted 'CEDAR VALLEY 8KM'. This spectacular road makes a beautiful, easy-surfaced walk, gently downwards at this stage, through fragrant pine woods.

Some **3.4km** along, where the road curves left, take the track off to the left (❶); if you miss it, go left on the road 400m/yds further on. Now you will experience stunning views to the south and west as your way curves gradually round to the east. After about **2h**, cedars will appear among the pine trees and become much more evident as you reach the area that gave rise to the name of **Cedar Valley**. You will come to a small PICNIC AREA with a water supply, close to a group of plane trees (❷; **2h30min**).

From here take the wide E4 track behind the barrier: first it heads north, then it dips south in a large hairpin. The track then heads north once more, and views open out all around. It's a gentle climb of 2km, and you may be lucky enough to spot a moufflon in the wild! Cedar trees are still very much in evidence as you approach the SUMMIT OF **Mount Tripylos** (❸; **3h30min**). From this peak (1362m/4470ft) there are magnificent views — eastward to Troodos, westward to the Akamas,

The forests around Stavros and Cedar Valley are in a healthier state now than they were in the early 1900s, and Winston Churchill can be credited for improving matters after 1907 when, as Under Secretary of State for the Colonies, he allocated funds for extensive tree-planting. The forests flourished in the ensuing years, but their welfare was not aided by the invading Turkish forces: in 1974 their air force needlessly set fire to over 150 square kilometres of trees. Recovery is continuing, thanks to the work of the Forestry Department.

and north to Morphou Bay. At the top there's a FIRE-WATCH STATION and a lovely small PICNIC AREA (Picnic 10).

From here it's a simple stroll of 2.5km back to **Dhodheka Anemi** (◯) and your car, reached in around **4h**. On a clear day the air could not have been fresher, nor the views more appealing.

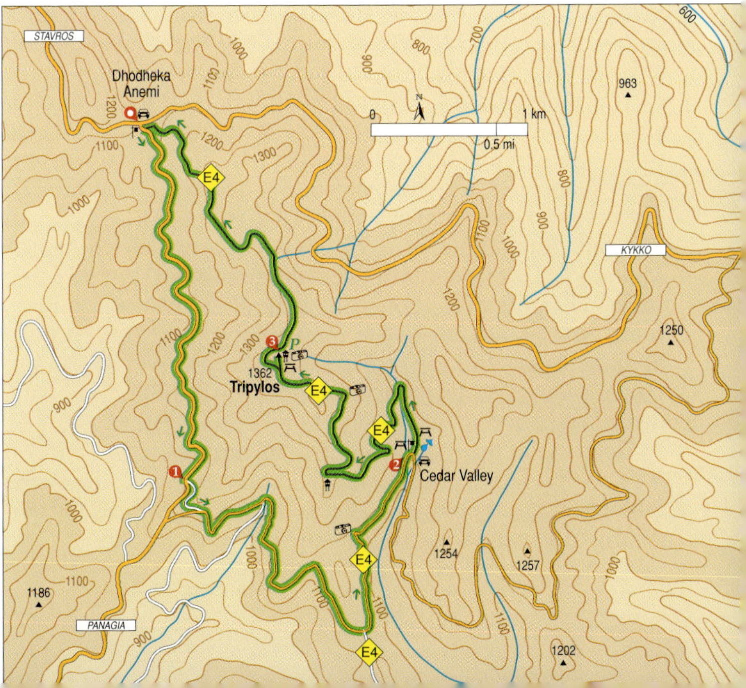

Walk 11: CIRCUIT FROM AGIOS NEOPHYTOS

Distance: 6.7km/4.2mi; 1h50min
Grade: ● moderate; steep initial ascent and steep final descent (250m/820ft overall) on a rough, (seasonally) overgrown path
Equipment: walking boots or stout shoes, sunhat, water, long trousers; optional trekking pole(s)
Transport: 🚗 car or taxi to/from Agios Neophytos (34° 50.763'N, 32° 26.825'E). Or 🚌 from Pafos (Timetable E9); return on the same bus from Tala (2km away). Or Pafos-Polis 🚌 (Timetable E5) to Tsadha, then 1km on foot: join the walk at the 1h-point and circle back to the same point.

The 12th-century monastery of St Neophytos is about 10km north of Pafos and dedicated to a man who was a noted scholar and writer, devoted man of God, and a hermit who chose a life of reclusion in caves that can still be seen by visitors. Some have beautiful frescoes that can be closely inspected, whether on a car outing or as a prelude to this circuit of the monastery valley.

Start out at the large **Agios Neophytos** CAR PARK (●) by walking back towards Pafos and *past* the turning for Tala. Just 80m/yds past the Tala turn-off (80m *before* an old stone warehouse with more recent extension), turn sharp left up a TRACK (❶). This rises fairly steeply (**5min**), but the effort is rewarded with ever-improving views over the monastery. Ignore a track off left and a grassy track right, then turn sharp left and either round three sides of an OLIVE GROVE or cut 60m straight across it — to a road (**15min**). Turn left uphill. When the road ends abruptly, climb a low bank, join another track and head up towards two houses. Meet another road and follow it left, past these houses, for 40m/yds, then head left on a track below the summit of **Melissovounos** (●). Ignoring a track off left, continue steadily uphill towards the radio aerials.

If you like, make a detour now of 300m/yds to the top, for views of Pafos and the coast. Otherwise, turn sharp left and follow the track uphill to the CREST (**45min**), from where it gently undulates. Ignore any turn-offs. The track, now tarmac, passes some houses and meets a quiet ROAD (❷; **1h**), where you turn left. After about 1km, by a bus stop, turn left on ARCHIP MAKARIOU III through a housing estate in **Koili**. Ignore a first street off right; after about 100m the street you are on bears right. At a T-junction, go left, then turn right on MAKADONIAS STREET. After 30m turn left downhill on a CONCRETE TRACK THROUGH VINEYARDS (❸; **1h20min**), with splendid views to the distant coast and the masts on Melissovounos ahead.

Keep to this main track, ignoring all turnings to the left. You soon see the Tala road across the valley to your right. After some 800m/half a mile on this concreted main track, it turns 90° left. At this point ignore a rocky path to the right. About 70m

As you rise at the start of the walk, there are fine views back to Agios Neophytos. Left: wall painting at the monastery

further on, just before a left-hand bend, turn sharp right down another TRACK (**4**; **1h30min**). This track ends some 300m/yds downhill (it used to make a hairpin bend to the right here, of which there may still be traces). Just to the left a ROCKY PATH (**5**) zigzags down to the monastery. It's obvious in summer, but may be overgrown in winter and spring. Follow this down to the WATER TANK, then the CAR PARK at **Agios Neophytos** (**O**; **1h50min**).

Walk 12: AROUND KATHIKAS

See also photo on page 25 **Distance:** 7.6km/4.7mi; 1h50min
Grade: ● easy (ascents/descents 150m/490ft), *but the nature trail is subject to mud slides: avoid the walk during or following wet weather.*
Equipment: walking boots or stout shoes, sunhat, water, picnic
Transport: 🚗 car to/from Kathikas (34° 54.722'N, 32° 25.546'E)
Short walk: Agiasma Nature Trail (3.5km/2.2mi; 1h; ● easy). Follow the main walk for 45min, then turn left at (❹), back to Kathikas.
Alternative walk: Akoursos (12km/7.4mi; 3h; ● easy, but with a return climb of 300m/980ft. At ❻ (1h08min) detour to **Akoursos**, an old village with a disused mosque, old olive press ... and spooky cemetery.

This walk, in an area developed by the Laona Project (see page 22) gives stunning views down a ravine full of jackdaws to the coast at Coral Bay. We then walk through vineyards, flushing partridge by the score.

Start from the CHURCH in **Kathikas** (●). Walk south on the signposted Akoursos road and after 250m/yds turn right on AGIASMATOS STREET, which soon bears left. After another 550m/yds, turn right on the **Agiasma Nature Trail** (❶; **15min**); it may be signposted. The rocky path descends past a turning to the 'official' start of the trail and comes to a bench at a SPRING (❷; **20min**; Picnic 12; photo on page 25). Take the path to the

Walk 12: Around Kathikas

right, cross the ravine and ascend under the cliffs, before contouring along the edge for a short way. Turn left on a track and, at the next SIGN (❸), turn left and zigzag up to another bench (**39min**), with a fine view to distant Coral Bay.

Continue to a dirt road and turn left to a crossroads (❹; **45min**). Turn right *(left for the Short walk)*, pass the chapel of **Agia Marina**, then stroll on to a T-junction with a concrete road (❺; **1h10min**). Turn left, in five minutes crossing the AKOURSOS ROAD (❻; *go right here for the Alternative walk*). Go straight over a crossing track 400m further on. After another 600m *turn sharp left* off the main track on a lesser track edging a vineyard (❼). Two minutes later go straight over a crossroads. In another two minutes go right at a Y-fork and ignore a sharp turning right after a little over 100m. Some 250m further on turn left. Ignore any tracks left or right until you come to a T-junction (❽; **1h35min**), where you turn right. After 200m turn left on a clear track; this bears left to the road (**1h40min**), where you turn right to **Kathikas** (**O**; **1h50min**).

The Agiasma nature trail starts innocently enough — a cart track through greenery. But the cliff walls seen in the background can be mudslides after rain.

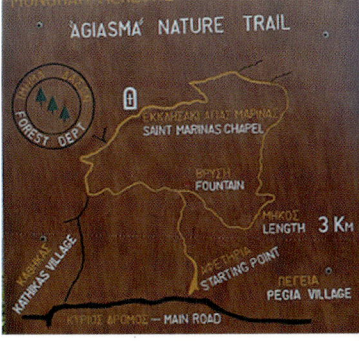

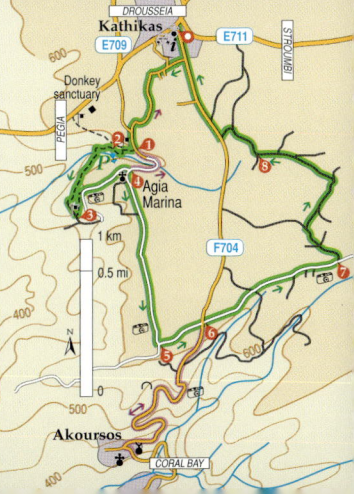

Walk 13: KISSONERGA TO CORAL BAY

Distance: 10km/6.2mi, 2h45min
Grade: ● easy, ascents of only 150m/490ft
Equipment: stout shoes, sunhat, water, picnic, swimming things
Transport: 🚗 car or taxi to Kissonerga; motorists can park near the sports ground or the church. Travelling by taxi, you could start at ❷ (the 30min-point), to avoid road-walking. Or 🚐 from Pafos (Timetable E7); alight at the sports ground. *To return:* 🚐 from Coral Bay to Pafos (Timetable E8), or to the junction of the Coral Bay/Kissonerga road, from where it is a 15min walk back to your car. Some buses return from Coral Bay to Pafos via Kissonerga (check at the tourist office or with Pafos Transport: see Timetable E8).

A few decades ago this ramble to the main irrigation reservoir of the Pafos region was marred by the intrusion of a military camp. But because it is so close to Pafos and so easy, it remains popular with 'Landscapers'.

The walk starts at **Kissonerga**, a village straddling the road between Pafos centre and Coral Bay. From the southern end of the SPORTS PITCH by the BUS STOP (**O**), walk north for 50m/yds or so, then turn right up APIS STREET (just before the PRIMARY SCHOOL on the right; it may be signposted to Tala). You pass the village CEMETERY, on your left, after about 180m/yds. Bear left at a roundabout and, at a T-junction (❶; **15min**), turn left. You are now heading almost due north, walking past fruit and vegetable plots.

About 1km past the T-junction, turn left on a track signposted to the VILLAS KIKLAMINO and KLATSOPATIKA and lined on the left with TALL CONIFERS (❷; **30min**). You will soon reach an area with a small WATER CONTROL POINT (❸) and a lane junction with signs left to the two aforementioned villas. Here your track swings right alongside a WATER CHANNEL on the

Above, right: citrus groves flourish in the valley below the Mavrokolymbos Dam. The dam is a key part of the irrigation system for the agricultural industry around Pafos. Below: Coral Bay

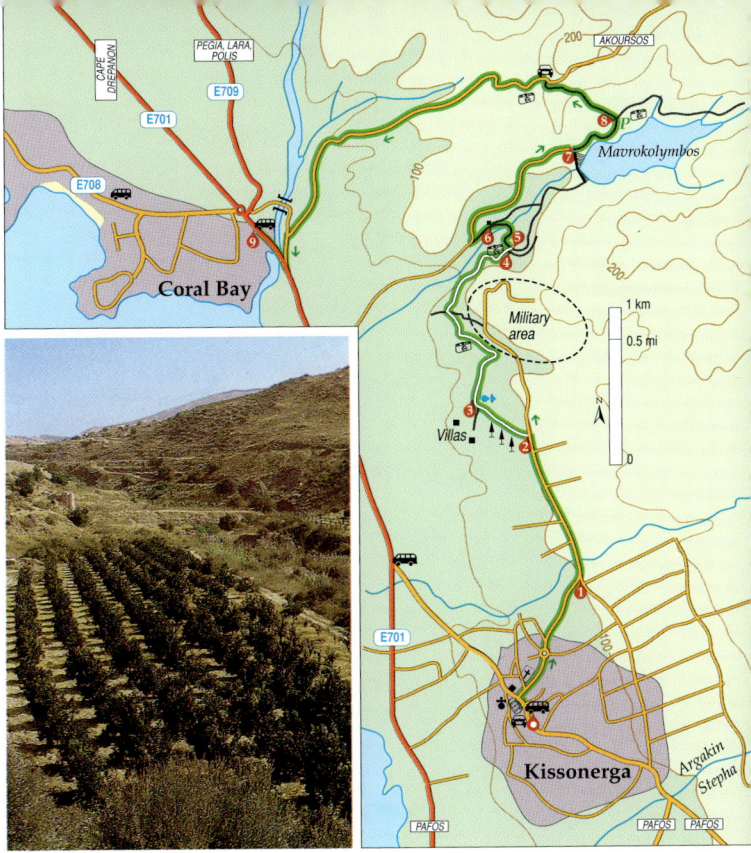

right (initially covered with concrete slabs). Follow this watercourse, with fine views over citrus groves as it heads inland.

At **50min** notice the cultivation below to your left and ignore a track to the right (**4**) as you skirt orange groves. Pass a LARGE GATE (**5**) just off to the right, as you head left along a fence on your right and zigzag down through orange trees. At a junction facing a SHED (**6**), turn left through the citrus trees, away from the dam. When you join the rough metalled SERVICE ROAD, turn sharp right uphill, climbing gently to the **Mavrokolymbos Dam** (**7**; Picnic 13; **1h25min**). Have a look at the steps, the sluice, a ruined building and an old bridge.

Then follow the track past the dam wall, and almost certainly see sheep and goats near the water's edge. About 500m beyond the dam wall, at a T-junction, turn left on a TRACK (**8**; **1h30min**) and climb to the AKOURSOS ROAD (**1h45min**). Turn left here, too: it's downhill almost all the way to the main E701 road. The nearest BUS STOP (**9**) is to the *right*, on the far side of the river, and buses are very frequent.

Or make for **Coral Bay** (**2h45min**) and take a dip!

Walk 14: LARA BEACH

See map overleaf; photo of Lara Beach on pages 14-15

Distance: 5.5km/3.4mi; 1h 20min

Grade: 🟢 easy; minimal ups and downs

Equipment: stout shoes, sunhat, water, picnic, swimming things

Transport: 🚗 car to/from the restaurant at Lara Beach (34° 56.671'N, 32° 18.872'E), 27km north of Pafos via Coral Bay. The road is asphalted as far as a U-bend at the Aspros River; it then reverts to a wide unsurfaced road. Just 1.1km further on you'll see the car park/info board for the Avagas Gorge on the right (Walk 16). After about 4km, beyond a sign to Lara Restaurant, the last 1km of track is very eroded — best done in a 4WD vehicle (or walked). Or ⛴ from Pafos (check at the tourist office for times)

Alternative walk (photo right): Avagas Gorge and Lara Beach (17.6km/11mi; 6h). 🟢 Quite easy, but long. Park at **Toxeftra**, at the signposted track to the Avagas Gorge (see 'Transport' above: 34° 55.128'N, 32° 19.673'E). Follow Walk 16 into the **Avagas Gorge**, to the narrowest point (❶) and then on to Lara and back. A great day out; worth putting the boots on!

Special note: Access may be restricted in July-August during the nesting season of the rare green turtle. Please observe relevant warning signs.

This attractive, unspoiled beach, setting for Picnic 14, can only be reached by car, or perhaps on a sea cruise out of Pafos during summer. By car it is a leisurely drive north, passing close to Coral Bay, then Agios Georgios. (A short detour here will show you an attractive fishing refuge and interesting church overlooking the sea.) The whole area dates back to Roman times.

Thankfully, Lara has been spared the ravages of commerce; much of the Akamas Peninsula was made a national park early in the 1990s, thus ensuring its continuing existence as an unspoiled landscape. One can tolerate and even give thanks for the single seasonal restaurant near the beach which caters for

most of Lara's visitors. Apart from the restaurant, there's absolutely nothing at Lara except wonderful coastal scenery and a quiet atmosphere. A most agreeable stroll can be made along and around the beach for an hour or two. Our map and GPS track is just a route suggestion; make your own way round the headland, passing the helipad (❶) and Info Centre (❷).

Start out near the LARA RESTAURANT (⭕) at **Lara Beach**, walking down to the shoreline. At the north end of the beach is a headland crossed by tracks, offering very pleasing views south along the coast and inland to the hills north of Pegia. Close to Lara are the summer nesting grounds of the rare and protected green turtle.

North of Lara, the rough road/E4 is even rougher before petering out after a few kilometres (see 4WD options for Car tour 1 on page 24), but there are some very secluded coves along here if you fancy skinny-dipping.

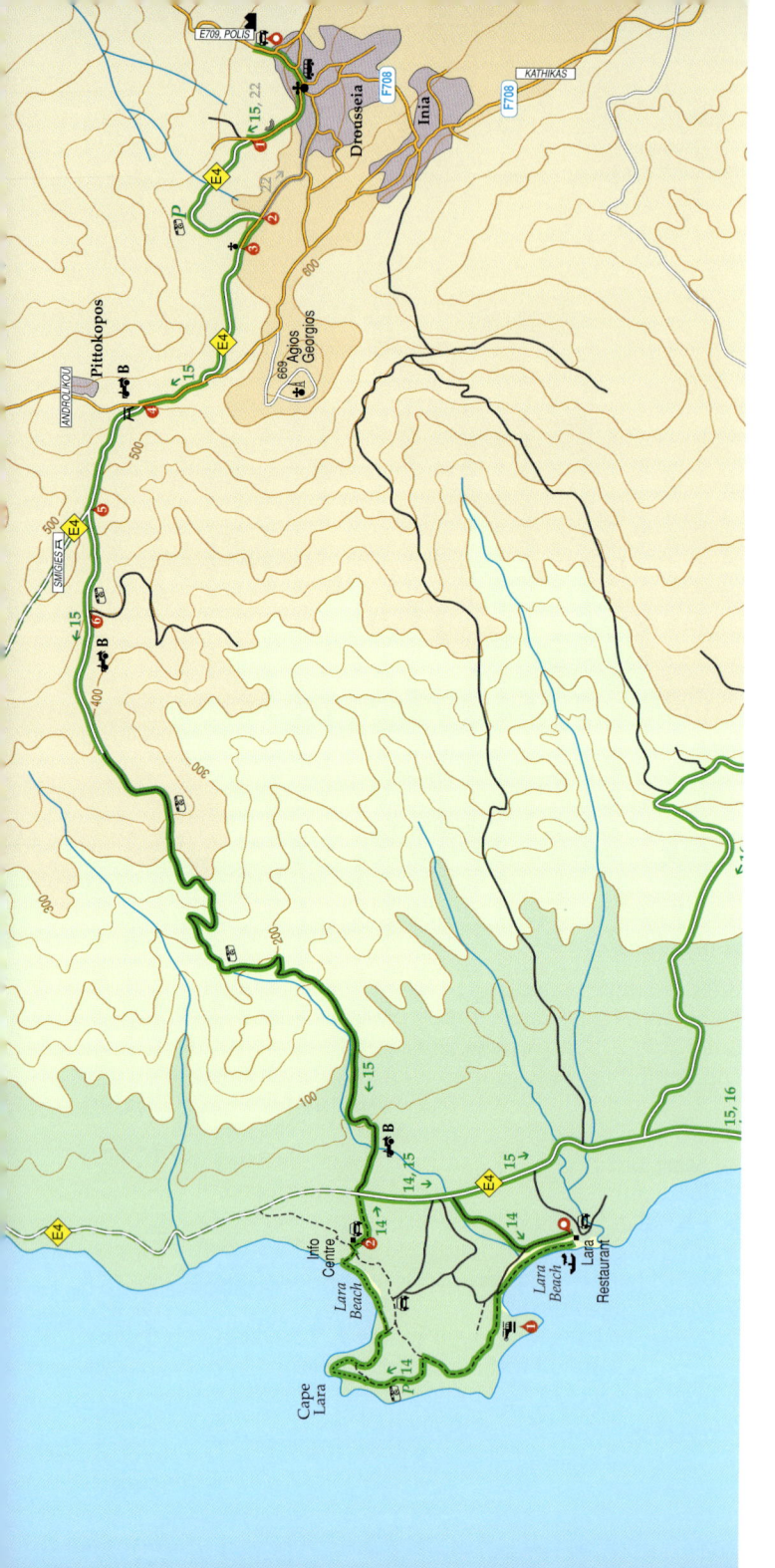

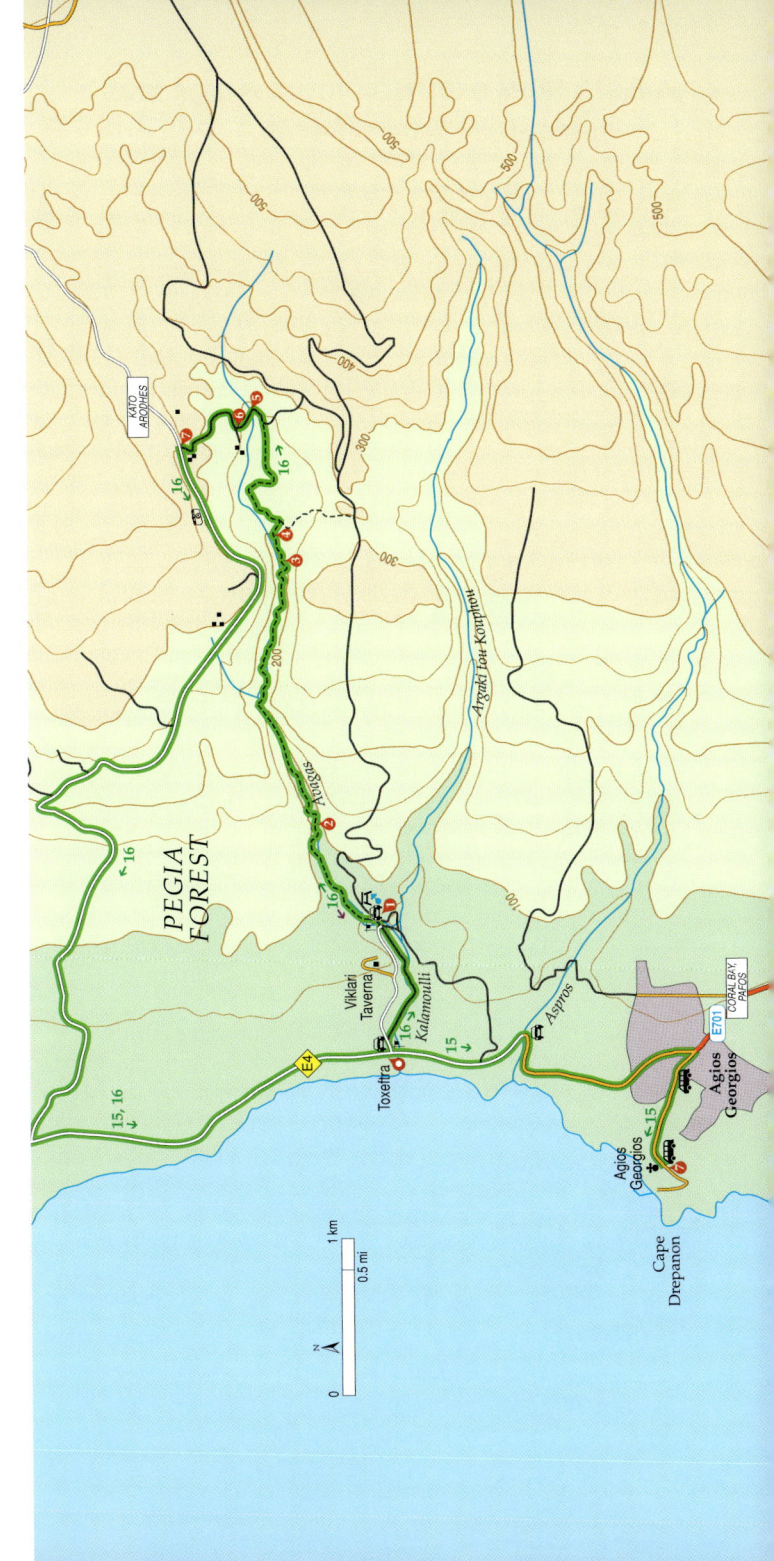

Walk 15: FROM DROUSSEIA TO AGIOS GEORGIOS

See map pages 82-83; see photos on pages 14-15, 80-81 and 86
Distance: 20km/12.4mi; about 5h
Grade: ● fairly easy but long, with a descent of 620m/2035ft
Equipment: walking boots or stout shoes, sunhat, plenty of water, picnic, swimming things
Transport: 🚌 to Polis (Timetable E5), then taxi to Drousseia (or with friends: 34° 57.815'N, 32° 23.937'E). *To return*: 🚌 from Agios Georgios (Timetable E6)
Alternative walks: Masochists can link up Walk 14 or Short walk 16.

In the cooler months of spring and autumn it's most enjoyable to take a long Cyprus walk. This trek is quite easy, but choose a coolish day and carry plenty of water. There are no facilities of any kind on the route. The good news is that much of the walk is level or downhill (albeit on rough tracks), and the views over the whole Lara coastline will linger long in the memory.

Start out from **Drousseia**: follow *Alternative* walk 22 on page 101. When you reach the T-JUNCTION (❷; **30min**), turn right (past the MODERN CHURCH; ❸) and keep going until you come to the asphalted Androlikou–Kathikas road. Turn right here and, 400m/yds further on, go left at a Y-FORK on a broad track (❹; **50min**); a SHELTER/VIEWPOINT will be on your right. You now follow the roughest 'road' you're likely to find on Cyprus (4WD Option B in Car tour 1 bumps along here). After 1km fork left (❺) and 550m/yds further on fork right (❻).

By now you are enjoying views over the whole western coast around Lara Bay which is slightly to the left on the horizon. That is your target! The way is simple, but don't rush it. Relish this *totally* unspoiled region, listen to the birdsong, smell the air, and take some wonderful photos as you follow the winding track gently downwards for some 7km, to join the rough E4 ROAD above **Lara Beach**.

After visiting the beach (Walk 14), you have another 7km of walking on a similar road —past the turn-off to the **Avagas Gorge** at **Toxeftra** (Walk 16). You should reach **Agios Georgios** CHURCH (❼) in under **5h**, depending on your stride, and how many times you stop to take in the scenery. You'll be tired and thirsty, but you'll thank me for this wonderful experience of the Akamas… although perhaps not immediately!

Seen en route in the Akamas: perils of not wearing a sunhat?

Walk 16: AVAGAS GORGE CIRCUIT

See map on pages 82-83; see also photo on pages 80-81
Distance: 14.8km/9.2mi, 5h20min
Grade: ●❗ moderate-strenuous and long, with an ascent/descent of 300m/1000ft. You must be sure-footed and agile: plenty of scrambling over slippery boulders as you criss-cross the stream bed; sometimes you'll need to use your hands. In winter the gorge may be *impassable,* if there is too much water. All year round there is a danger of rockfall, so a safety helmet is advisable. A good sense of direction is a help as you leave the gorge for the plateau above, and the long return on the *shadeless* motor track is tiring, especially in hot weather.
Equipment: walking boots, sunhat, *plenty of* water, picnic, swimwear
Transport: 🚗 via Agios Georgios, north of Pafos. Continue on track when the asphalt runs out 1.6km past Agios Georgios, and park 1.1km further on at a sign for the gorge at Toxeftra (34° 55.128'N, 32° 19.673'E). Or 🚌 to/from Agios Georgios (Timetable E6), then 2.7km on foot
Short walk: Avagas Gorge (2km/1.2mi; 1h; ●❗ fairly easy, but you *must* be sure-footed and agile). Access as above, but turn right at the Toxeftra car park and keep ahead on the track, passing the drive up left to the Viklari Taverna after 550m, then turn left between two gateposts 400m further on, to a second car park with a noticeboard (34° 55.226'N, 32° 20.277'E). Follow the main walk from the 15min-point to ❶ and back.

It's easy enough to venture into the Avagas Gorge from its mouth, walking only as far in as you feel comfortable (Short walk), but this circuit takes you up to the Laona Plateau for the beautiful views shown overleaf.

Start out at the **Toxeftra** CAR PARK (**O**) on the coastal road. Walk up the track for just 40m/yds, then turn right on a path through long grass; a fence is on your right. You cross and recross the river bed and eventually come to a second parking area (❶; **15min**; *Short walk starting point*). Walk past a BARRIER to the left, into the northerly and most spectacular of the two ravines here, the **Avagas Gorge**. A set of shallow steps takes you into the gorge proper, flowing with water and where rock walls tower above you, cutting out the sun. Clambering round and over boulders, you pass the NARROWEST POINT (❷; **45min**), where the gorge walls are just 3-4m apart. Beyond here, some CAIRNS AND RED PAINT DAUBS help with orientation, as you walk beside and in the stream bed. Birds and lizards abound, and you may spot a snake in hot weather. You *will* see a WRECKED TRUCK at the left of the path…

About 15 minutes past the wreck you pass a POST MARKED '48' (❸; **2h05min**). Keep ahead for a good 100m/yds, then take a narrow goats' path on the right (❹; CAIRN/RED PAINT), to rise up out of the gorge. At the top, head left at the T-junction with a wide grassy path at the southern edge of the gorge. The grassy path becomes an earthen road and meets a fork (❺; **2h20min**) go left downhill here, cross the stream bed and emerge on the north side of the gorge. As the track widens out, turn right at another fork as you approach a GOAT FARM (❻). Walk on up to join the unsurfaced road between Lara and Kato Arodhes at a T-junction (**7**) and turn left.

You enjoy some splendid views from the high point of this motorable track. Ignore a lesser track off right, pass another GOAT FARM and, ignoring all turn-offs, just keep to the unsurfaced road as it descends through the **Pegia Forest**. At the T-junction with the E4 unsurfaced coastal road (**4h20min**), turn left and walk back to the PARKING AREA at **Toxeftra** (O; **5h20min**).

On the plateau above the Avagas Gorge

Walk 17: KHAPOTAMI GORGE

Distance: 10.3km/6.4mi; 2h35min

Grade: ● moderate, basically a descent of 200m/650ft... but it can be extremely hot in the gorge in high summer. *In early spring the walk may be impassable if there has been heavy rain and the river is running high.*

Equipment: walking boots or stout shoes, sunhat, *plenty of water*, picnic

Transport: 🚌 (Timetable E10) or 🚕 taxi/friends from Pafos to Pano Arkhimandrita; alight at the bus stop at the top of the village. *To return:* 🚕 pre-arranged taxi from Alekhtora, or take the village taxi to the main road at Pissouri and telephone a service taxi bound for Pafos or Lemesos.

Circular walk for motorists: Khapotami Gorge from Kato Arkhimandrita (9.3km/5.8mi; 2h30min; ● moderate; *the gorge may be impassable in winter/spring* and, after gentle undulations, the ascent of 150m/500ft at the end of the walk, in full sun, should *be avoided in summer*). 🚗 car to Pano Arkhimandrita as above. After viewing the SHRINE (❶), drive back west to the VILLAGE WATER TANK and turn left for 'KATO ARKHIMANDRITA 2KM', to drive down the narrow, rough road to **Kato Arkhimandrita** and park by the CHURCH (34° 44.177′N, 32° 40.801′E). Pick up the main walk at ❷ and follow it to ❻. Turn left here and walk up a gravel road towards an ELECTRICITY PYLON. Take it easy on this long climb in full sun. After passing to the right of the pylon, be sure to keep to the main track: at ⓐ veer right (northeast) uphill at a Y-fork and follow the track as it bends left (northwards), ignoring a fork to the right; 130m/yds further on, at ⓑ, again keep right. There is nothing to distinguish the brow of the hill (ⓒ) — a mere bump in the track and a sense of briefly levelling off before you head downhill, back to the CHURCH at **Kato Arkhimandrita** (❷; 2h30min).

Pano Arkhimandrita is situated among vineyards perched on hillsides, and the effect of the scenery when you first arrive is quite breathtaking. There is more to come.

Clearly signed by the village BUS STOP (◯) is a concrete road to 'THE CAVE OF 318 FATHERS'. Follow this and then go down some steps to the recently restored hermitage of **Agii Pateres** (❶), a tiny SHRINE nestling in a rock crevice. Herein is preserved a quantity of human bones. It is said they are of 318 saints who arrived on the coast at Pissouri in days of yore after fleeing persecution in Syria, only to meet an untimely death at the hands of local heathens. Your welcome in Arkhimandrita will be warmer, especially in either of the two coffee shops where locals will happily talk about their tiny community.

Visit the SHRINE shown on page 89 (respecting the 'don't touch' appeal), and admire the well-preserved frescoes, then **begin the walk** by scrambling down the slope alongside the telegraph pole to the dirt track just below. Follow this to the right as it hugs the side of the hill, ending just below the village CHURCH on a concrete road (**10min**). Turn right here and then almost immediately left on the F612, heading downhill. After 400m/yds, by the VILLAGE WATER TANK, turn left on a road signed to 'KATO ARKHIMANDRITA' (**15min**).

A couple of minutes down this road, at a crossroads with

a telegraph pole, turn left and continue downhill, with the **Arkhimandrita Valley** on your left. When you reach the village of **Kato Arkhimandrita** (❷; **40min**) you'll see that it's mostly abandoned to the goats, but a couple of the houses — and the church — have been restored. The inhabitants asked

to leave and move to the upper village in the 1960s, because of their isolation (no good road, no school) and water supply problems.

Above, from left to right: the priest at Pano Arkhimandrita when I first wrote this book and a wall painting inside his church; church in the ruined village of Kato Arkhimandrita and the shrine at the start of the walk.
Left: Arkhimandrita's green valley

Walk through the village. Fork left in front of a RESTORED HOUSE (**3**) at the next Y-fork, and cross over the (usually dry) river bed at a FORD (**4**; **49min**). At the crossroads on the far side of the river bed, take the track to the right. As you head down into the river bed, the wind turbines on the hill to the right almost disappear from view.

Follow the track along the valley floor as you head into the spectacular **Khapotami Gorge**. Towering cliffs, birds of prey wheeling overhead, an infinite variety of trees and plants, lizards scampering at your feet ... the holiday beaches seem a long way from this kind of Cyprus. Follow the 'track' — sometimes just the boulders of the river bed *(and totally impassable when the river is running high in*

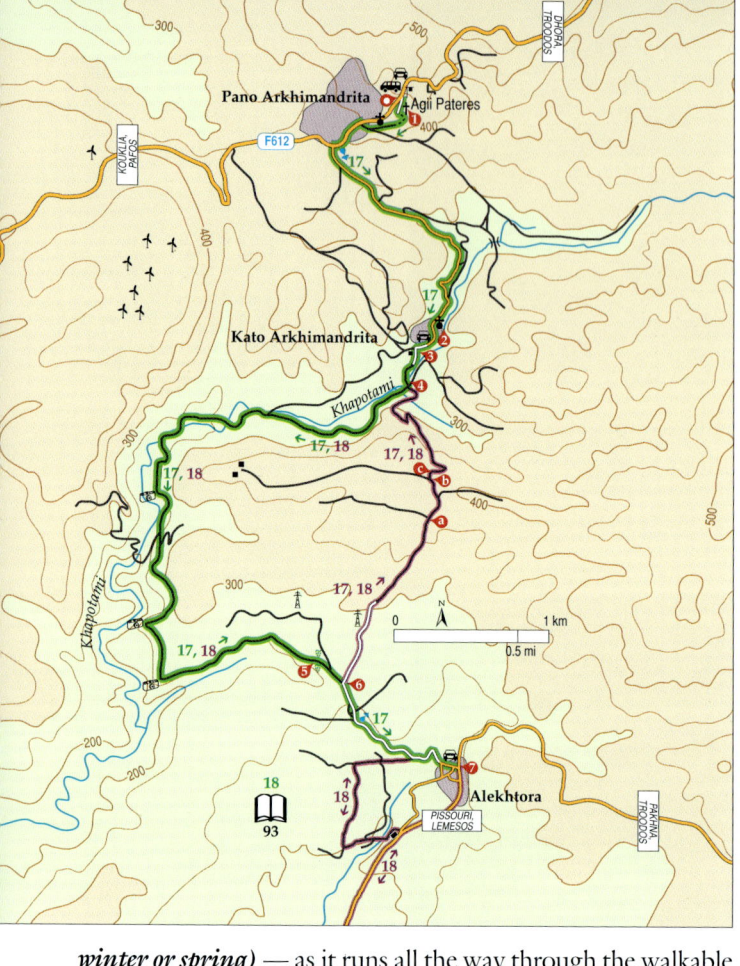

winter or spring) — as it runs all the way through the walkable part of the gorge. After about **1h30min**, the track emerges into an open area on the valley floor, and from this point you will begin to climb steadily. You will get ever more impressive views down into the impassable part of the gorge as you climb.

Eventually, the track levels out and contours round two sharp left-hand bends: the Khapotami Gorge is on your right after the first 90° bend and the gorge of an unnamed tributary follows the second bend to the left. The way is mostly contouring but rises gently to pass through a VINEYARD (**5**), followed by an OLIVE GROVE.

The track then passes between pine trees and immediately comes to a junction (**6**; **2h20min**) where you go straight ahead. *(But for the Circular walk, turn left here on the gravel road.)* Now it's just somewhat over 1km to the main road at **Alekhtora** (**7**; **2h35min**), where your taxi should be waiting.

Walk 18: CIRCUIT FROM ALEKHTORA

Distance: 8.6km/5.3mi; 2h20min — or shorten by almost 4km/50min by parking the antenna at the 50min-point (34° 41.797'N, 32° 39.608'E). The approach to the antenna is just about passable in an ordinary car.
Grade: ● quite easy, with a climb/descent of about 150m/490ft overall, but it helps to have a good sense of direction (or a compass/GPS)
Equipment: walking boots or stout shoes, sunhat, water, picnic, compass
Transport: 🚗 take the F611 north from Pissouri to the junction near the sign 'Alekhtora 1km', where the road makes a near-90° right turn, next to a fruit-packing factory (34° 41.850'N, 32° 40.400'E; see map on page 93).

Alternative walk: Alekhtora — Lakko tou Frankou — Khapotami Gorge — Alekhtora (24.4km/15.1mi; 6h40min; ● strenuous and long, with ascents/descents of about 400m/1300ft overall). Equipment and access as main walk; take *plenty of water. Not suitable in high summer,* as there is almost no shade. Combine this walk with Walk 17 for a very long day out. After this walk (for which see map overleaf), head north along the road towards Alekhtora for 1km (now using the map opposite). Then, just past a disused fruit-packing shed on the left, fork left on a track running behind the back of the shed, ignoring the narrow road to the right. Ignore a track off right; take the *next* track to the right, 500m/yds from the shed. Skirting vineyards on the right, head north for 600m/yds. Then, at a T-junction, turn right for 400m/yds, to meet the vehicle track followed at the end of Walk 17. Turn left here, and after 0.8km/half a mile turn right on a gravel road. This is Waypoint ⑥ of Circular walk 17: pick up those notes above the map on page 87 ('Turn left here and walk up a gravel road…'). Follow that circuit to **Kato Arkhimandrita** (❷). Then use the notes for Walk 17 from the 40min-point, to walk through the **Khapotami Gorge** and back to **Alekhtora**, picking up your outward track round the vineyards and turning right at the disused fruit-packing shed, back to your car.

This is an interesting walk, mainly through farming land. The old hamlet of Lakko tou Frankou provides a fascinating insight into life past and, if you haven't already done Walk 17, the spectacular views into the gorge will surely whet your appetite for it.

Start out at the junction by the 'ALEKHTORA' sign (⓿). Follow a surfaced track northwest through vineyards and a few olive groves. Go straight on at a junction (**12min**), still gently climbing. You pass another fruit-packing depot and an ENCLOSURE sheltering goats with with longest, floppiest ears you're ever likely to see! The track soon starts zigzagging up to the antenna visible above. Make use of short-cuts and reach the

Agios Georgios and, to its left, the khan *at Lakko tou Frankou*

top at the solar-powered ANTENNA (❶; **30min**, Picnic 18a). Have a breather, if not a picnic, and survey the countryside you have just traversed.

Follow another track northwest uphill past the antenna. As you can see on the map, we're heading for an overview of the Khapotami Gorge, the setting for Walk 17. Goats graze amongst the carob trees, and large flocks of jackdaws screech noisily. After a few minutes, some 150m/yds short of a large ENCLOSURE OF GOAT SHEDS (❷; **40min**), bear left: take the track running westwards, walking through carob trees and keeping the large wind turbines above the gorge to your right. After five minutes, bear left at a minor junction and you will see, above the trees on the distant hillside ahead, a large animal farm with a feed silo on the roof. Head for this; always keep the wind turbines on your right. When you reach the ANIMAL FARM (**1h**), take the track which heads down along its left-hand side. Step down through old stone terraces to the KHAPOTAMI OVERLOOK (❸; **1h10min**; Picnic 18b), for really spectacular views into the Khapotami Gorge.

When you have enjoyed a break in these beautiful surroundings, return a little way towards the farm and, standing with your back to both the farm and the ridge (facing SSE), look for a clear vehicle track that runs initially to the left of and then turns into the sparse pine woods. Follow this track (❹) past a tall TRIANGULATION POINT painted with a large number '9' on your right. Continue to follow the track south downhill. The rough track descends and takes you to the tiny church shown on the previous page, **Agios Georgios** (❺; **1h30min**). It has white walls, a blue roof (when last seen) and no windows.

Immediately beyond the church is an 18th-century

Goat enclosure typical of the island's interior

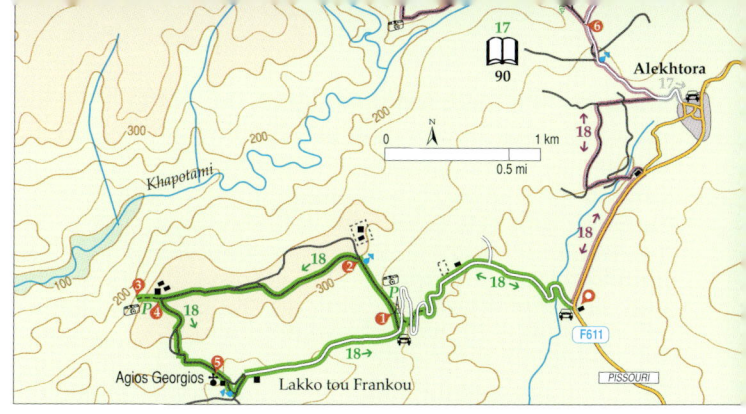

'KHAN' or coaching station. Just beyond this the track comes to a junction, where a stone trough sits beside an OLD WELL (now dry). This perhaps gave rise to this area's name of **Lakko tou Frankou** (Well of the French). Turn sharp left at this junction and in two minutes pass a RIDING CLUB on your right. The vehicle track rises gradually (it used to be cobbled in places, indicating that this was perhaps an important trans-village link in bygone days). When you reach the antenna junction of your outward route (**1h55min**), don't forget the short-cuts for your descent. Say 'hello' to the long-eared goats and return to your car at the 'ALEKHTORA' sign (**O**; **2h20min**).

Walk 19: FONTANA AMOROSA COASTAL TRAIL

See map on reverse of touring map; see also photo on pages 96-97
Distance: 12km/7.4mi, 3h30min
Grade: ● quite easy, almost level walking
Equipment: stout shoes, sunhat, water, picnic, swimming things
Transport: 🚌 car or 🚐 (Timetable F1) to/from Lakki, then either ⛴ or 🚙 jeep service to Fontana Amorosa
Short walk: Cape Arnauti (6km/3.7mi, 1h45min; grade, equipment and transport as main walk). Just do the first part of the walk and return from **Fontana Amorosa** by boat or jeep.

This is a wonderful walk with amazing views around the compass. Birdsong, butterflies, tiny lizards avoiding your feet, and a backdrop of mountains. What more could one ask for? This walk takes you through unspoiled Cyprus, and long may it remain so. In reality the 'fountain of love' is a 5-metre deep well (which you may not even find), but it doesn't matter! You have only come for the pleasure of walking back to the Baths of Aphrodite. For a longer ramble, it is interesting to walk to the very western tip of the island, Cape Arnauti (an extra 3km/2mi return), passing the wrecked freighter Agnello.

In the past, the only approach to Fontana Amorosa was from the sea. A few years ago some entrepreneurs started a half-hourly jeep service. Sharing a boat or jeep with others will ensure that the cost is very reasonable. On the negative side, while the frequent jeeps greatly simplify logistics for walkers wanting to save time … like jeep safaris, they interrupt the peace with noise and trail dust in their wake. By sea, there is no proper landing area; the boatman asks you to leap ashore on a hot and rocky outcrop which, at first sight, hardly merits its name.

Start out at the SIGNBOARD for the **Fontana Amorosa** area (⭕): follow the track in a northwesterly direction, but always keep to paths nearest to the sea. You'll pass the scant, rusted remains of a freighter that came to grief many years ago and eventually come to a SHRINE at the most westerly point on the island, **Cape Arnauti** (❶; **45min**). If you are only doing the Short walk, you'll have plenty of time to potter around the Cape beyond the shrine; the rest of us head back the same way to **Fontana Amorosa** (⭕; **1h30min**).

Now simply head eastwards along the E4 track and enjoy the environment. Although the track wanders through scrub on both sides, you should soon be enjoying good views of the sea. About 20 minutes along you come to a large WARNING SIGN about military exercises and take good notice: don't touch anything suspicious-looking. Equally, don't be deterred by the 'red flag' aspect of this walk, with no evidence of the military, except for the signs.

Walk 19: Fontana Amorosa coastal path

Some 20 minutes later, after turning inland very briefly to avoid a gully, the track gains height. Five minutes later you may catch sight of a cairn on a rock to the right and spot a particularly attractive cove down left (❷; **2h20min**). Eventually the route climbs more steeply, but not for long, and the views from this level are the finest of the walk. At the end of this stretch, you have a panoramic view over your destination. For this last descent, keep to the broader track on the right, not the narrower way through low-lying trees... lest you disturb the goats as you drop down to the **Baths of Aphrodite** (**3h30min**).

From the Baths you can probably catch a jeep shuttle back to Lakki, or you can call for a taxi when you arrive. If you've not left a car at Lakki, you can catch a bus direct back to Polis.

One of the delightfully secluded coves passed en route, seen from above the Baths of Aphrodite; the camping site is nicely situated on the cliffs in the background.

Walk 20: THE 'APHRODONIS' TRAIL

See map on reverse of touring map; see also photos on pages 95 and 99 (bottom)

Distance: about 7.5km/4.7mi; 2h50min, whichever trail you choose

Grade: ● moderate, with a steep climb of 250m/820ft at the start. The Aphrodite Trail climbs an additional 100m/330ft. Both trails involve zigzag descents on fairly loose rubble in places; *you must be sure-footed and have a head for heights.*

Equipment: stout shoes or walking boots, sunhat, water, picnic; optional trekking pole(s), swimming things

Transport: 🚗 car or taxi to/from the Baths of Aphrodite restaurant car park (35° 3.366'N, 32° 20.823'E). Or 🚌 from Polis (Timetable F1)

Walkers who have trod the Fontana Amorosa coastal path (Walk 19) know how special the views are in this 'top left-hand corner' of Cyprus. Imagine how much more exciting those views are from 300 metres (1000 feet) higher up! Thanks to a pair of Forestry Department nature trails ('Aphrodite' and 'Adonis'), you can enjoy these views and at the same time learn more about the flora and fauna of the Akamas. A booklet explaining points of interest, and a large-scale map, are usually available from the Polis tourist office.

Walk 20: The 'Aphrodonis' Trail 97

The two trails share a common ascent at the start, lasting a little over an hour. The Aphrodite Trail then heads northwest, climbing to skirt the Moutti tis Sotiras plateau, and offers incomparable views towards Cape Arnauti. The Adonis Trail heads in the opposite direction initially, giving splendid views over the coastline southeast of the Baths of Aphrodite. I take you up to the 'decision point', then describe both trails. Whichever you choose, you're likely to come back and head the opposite way another day!

You need more than sandals or trainers for either experience, for while the routes are well marked and by no means severe, they do present some challenge to wind and limb, and the surfaces can be rocky or loose, especially on their zigzag descents (some 'Landscapers' have experienced mild vertigo on the Aphrodite descent).

The walk starts at the CAR PARK (**O**) close to the CTO RESTAURANT. Head west to the clearly signed start to the trails. You reach **Loutra Aphroditis** (**❶**; the **Baths of Aphrodite**) at TRAIL POINT 5; Aphrodite was said to sport with lovers here.

Follow the sign 'NATURE TRAIL', crossing the bed of the **Argaki tou Pyrgou** and heading up steps. The coastal track from Fontana Amorosa (Walk 19), your return route, is below. Go through a turnstile and look up left to see two WHITE CONCRETE CAIRNS; head sharp left up to the highest cairn (painted with the number '2'. Keeping this to your right, follow the steep path to a third cairn — at TRAIL POINT 8 (**15min**). Keep left at another fork two minutes later.

As you rise, you'll notice a small island with a cross, which commemorates a diver who lost his life near the island some years ago. About 50m past TRAIL POINT 10 you are directed sharply up to the right, and you very soon come to TRAIL POINT 11. There are seats near here from where you can enjoy your first really good views

Cape Arnauti from the initial ascent on the 'Aphrodonis Trail' (Picnic 20)

over the coast (**2**; **35min**; Picnic 20, photo on pages 96-97). Walk through a clearing which is level for about 200m/yds, but ahead you'll see (and feel!) the trail rising sharply. It can be a sweat, but the pain doesn't last long! At the top there's a welcome bench, from which to look back to Lakki and beyond to Polis.

At a fork beyond TRAIL POINT 20 turn left (**3**). You will come to a large wooded hollow with a GIANT OAK TREE and the substantial remains of **Pyrgos tis Rigaenas** (**4**; Queen's Shelter; **1h10min**, photograph opposite, below), believed to be the site of a medieval monastery. Nearby is a welcome SPRING (but it *may* be dry in summer). This is another excellent area for picnicking (Picnic 20), while you decide which of the trails to follow — **Aphrodite or Adonis**; both are signposted from the hollow (as is another nature trail, Smigies, which is followed in Walk 21).

Aphrodite (A25 to A49): Follow the signposted track which rises in a northwesterly direction. After TRAIL POINT A30 leave the track on a short-cut path to the right, passing a flourish of rock roses. Following signs, zigzag up to TRAIL POINT A35. (If you continue a few yards up the track here, a path from the vehicle turning area leads to a viewpoint on the **Moutti tis Sotiras** plateau.) But you will have equally stunning view towards Cape Arnauti from TRAIL POINT A37 (**a**), as you zigzag down the narrowing path. *Take care* where the surface is loose. You join the coastal track from Fontana Amorosa at around **2h20min** and pass another SPRING a few minutes later. After a short climb you finish up back at the RESTAURANT at the **Baths of Aphrodite** (**O**; **2h50min**). This is a marvellous walk at any time of year, but in spring you may have the bonus of spotting the Cyprus tulip.

Adonis (B25 to B55): The trail climbs a short distance, past juniper trees. Near POINT B29 you briefly join a FORESTRY ROAD (**b**); keep left downhill. Beyond a fine stand of Calabrian pines (TRAIL POINT B30), keep left downhill on a PATH (**c**), leaving the track. When you come to TRAIL POINT B34 (**d**; **1h45min**), turn left (the way straight ahead also leads to the Smigies Trail and Walk 21). There's a WATER TROUGH here, of alleged drinking quality, but you may prefer your bottle. There's a really lovely descent now, to the right of a gully, and the whole area is covered with wild flowers in spring. Simply follow the trail numbers (there's a long gap between B46 and B47). At TRAIL POINT B50 you come to a stunning VIEWPOINT (**e**) with a bench, from where you can see your zigzag descent. At the bottom, turn left on the road, back to the **Baths of Aphrodite** (**O**; **2h50min**).

Walk 21: AKAMAS GOLD

Map on reverse of touring map; see also photo on page 17
Distance: 13km/8mi; 3h30min
Grade: ● moderate, with ascents of about 250m/820ft
Equipment: walking boots or stout shoes, sunhat, water, picnic, *torch*
Transport: 🚗 car, friends or taxi to/from Neo Chorio (35° 1.531'N, 32° 21.823'E); there are also buses from Polis, but times are inconvenient.

Short walk for motorists: Smigies Nature Trail (6.5km/4mi; 2h; ● easy). Drive on the rough road out of Neo Chorio to the Smigies picnic site (35° 1.440'N, 32° 19.993'E; see map) and start and end the walk there.

Even shorter walk for motorists: ● Do the Short walk above, but turn off the ridge track at nature trail signpost No 9 (**5**), where there is a sign 'SMIGIES 2KM — SHORT WAY'.

Alternative walks: Below are just two possibilities from the many walk options in this area (see map on reverse of touring map). Take a taxi to start; return from the Baths by 🚌 (Timetable F1).

1 Neo Chorio — Smigies — Aphrodite Trail — Baths of Aphrodite (13km/8mi; 3h15min; ● grade as main walk, but with an additional climb of 100m/330ft). After visiting the MINE (1h30min), retrace your steps to the ridge track, continue along it, then turn right at a military warning sign to join the **Aphrodite Trail** (Walk 20) near trail point A35. Pick up the notes on page 98 to climb round the **Moutti tis Sotiras** plateau and then descend to the **Baths** (**O**). (You could also turn *right* on the trail, to descend more directly via **Pyrgos tis Rigaenas** (**4**).

2 Neo Chorio — Smigies — Adonis Trail — Baths of Aphrodite (10km/6.2mi; 2h30min; ● grade as main walk). From the MINE (**4**), continue on the Smigies Nature Trail, then join the **Adonis Nature Trail** near point B34 (**d**). Keep ahead to descend to the **Baths** (**O**).

Is it a gold mine? Or was it just magnesium ore that Cypriot miners extracted from the abandoned mine workings we find on this grand route? Let's go see, but don't give up the day job yet! The real rewards on this day's outing are the magnificent views over Chrysochou (Golden) Bay and the Akamas Forest in the south.

Start out at the CHURCH in **Neo Chorio** (**O**). Walk west along the road to some WATER TANKS on the edge of the village, just beyond which the road forks (**1**; **10min**). Head right here,

Some say this abandoned mine once produced gold… but old maps indicate magnesium. Whatever the end product, this is the old smelter, opposite the galleried workings of the mine. Below: Pyrgos tis Rigaenas (Alternative walk and Walk 20)

towards 'Agios Minas'. The left fork would take you to the goats of Androlikou (see page 24)… another day, perhaps? Beyond the restored church of **Agios Minas** (**40min**) the concrete road reverts to track and you come to the popular **Smigies** PICNIC SITE (❷; **50min**; Picnic 21). Keep to the left of it*, passing the start of a signposted circuit round the **Pissouromouti** peak. (This optional detour, including a climb to the top, would give you a magnificent view over the whole coast: allow 3km/2mi and an extra 125m/400ft of ascent; 1h.)

Come at **55min** to a T-junction of tracks on a ridge ('Route A' in the 4WD Options for Car tour 1 on page 24). Turn right and start enjoying the views, firstly to the left, and later, in both directions. There'll likely be a welcome breeze, even on a hot day. You pass the turn-off to a FIRE-WATCH STATION, then come to a signpost back to 'SMIGIES 2KM — SHORT WAY' (❸) on your right *(the 'Even shorter walk')*. Having joined the **Smigies Nature Trail**, keep ahead for 500m/yds, to a level track on the right rounding the hillside. *Ignore* this but, 150m further on, turn right on a track marked with a GREEN ARROW. It drops sharply to the right, passes a large ruined shelter on the left and leads to the ABANDONED MINES (❹; **1h30min**). On the left is the SMELTING FURNACE (what's left of it), ahead is a short-cut to your ongoing path and, to the right, entrances to the old galleries. *If you have a torch*, you might explore for a short way, but take care (there are deep pits inside!), and don't venture in alone.

You now have several options.

For the main walk, walk back a few paces and follow the track that descends to the left of the smelter (GREEN ARROW) then, at TRAIL POINT 14 (turpentine tree), turn hard right (almost back the way you came) and follow the path gently uphill. Soon you join a track and can see the church of Agios Minas ahead to the left. The track leads back to the PICNIC SITE (**2h40min**), from where you can retrace your steps to **Neo Chorio** (**3h30min**).

For Alternative walk 1, return to the ridge track as described above, to reach the **Aphrodite Trail** northwest of Pyrgos tis Rigaenas, then see notes on page 98.

For Alternative walk 2 continue as the main walk, but keep *left* past TRAIL POINT 14, to reach the **Adonis Trail** near a SPRING (**Kefalovrisia**) and SIGNPOST B34; then see notes on page 98.

A great day's walking, whatever your choice of routes.

---

*My route picks up the Smigies Nature Trail at point 9; if you prefer to follow the route from the start, walk down into the picnic site to join the path (shown in yellow on the map) at the left of the trail sign.

Walk 22: TWO AKAMAS VILLAGES

Walk a: Kritou Terra and the Kremiotis Waterfalls (5.2km/3.2mi, 1h45min;
● moderate, with a *sometimes steep and uneven* descent/re-ascent of about 230m/750ft, demanding agility. You visit two waterfalls, one of them accessible either via a *claustrophobic* tunnel in the rock beneath a waterfall (you get soaked) or a new bridge… Wear bathing things, lace-up swim shoes, sunhat; take towel, plastic bag (to wrap up camera and phone!), picnic, water. 🚗 to/from Kritou Terra (a detour on Car tour 1; there are buses from both Pafos and Polis, but timings are inconvenient). Park near the springs at the entrance to the village (⊙; 34° 57.278'N, 32° 25.154'E). A small fee is charged for path maintenance.

Walk b: Drousseia circuit (3.5km/2.2mi; 1h; ● easy, with an ascent/descent of just 40m/130ft). 🚗 to Drousseia (there are buses from both Pafos and Polis, but timings are inconvenient); park behind the Droushia Heights Hotel (⊙; 34° 57.815'N, 32° 23.937'E). Notes below.

Walk a is a stunner, but a bit taxing in hot weather. It visits not only a charming village but a 'secret' waterfall that became an Instagram hit among the local populace during the pandemic … when there were half-hour queues to see the falls! We still don't advise visiting on a weekend. Walk b is an ideal leg-stretcher, all on concrete and tarmac and suitable for sandals.

Start Walk a at the entrance to **Kritou Terra** (⊙): take the middle road, between the SPRINGS (left) and an old MILLSTONE (right). Midway through the village, as the road bends up right, you reach a large BLUE SIGNBOARD indicating the way to a number of points of interest. Leave the main road here and FORK LEFT (❶) towards St George's church and the waterfall, amongst others. (A right leads to the church shown overleaf.) On the left here is the vine-covered former FLOUR MILL. *Do* look over the low wall beyond it, to see a series of holes in the rock beside a water channel — the old COMMUNAL LAUNDRY.

At the end of the village, you pass the CHURCH and a road right to an Environmental Studies Centre (attracting 2000 international students each year). Keep on this road to 'THE WATERFALLS', ignoring any offshoots, for just under 1km — to where it becomes a motor track and curves down to a fee-paid CAR PARK (❷). A shady trail begins here and runs to the UPPER **Kremiotis Waterfall** (❸; **35min**), where there's a decent-sized POOL and a PICNIC AREA (Picnic 22a).

A newer nature trail starts here, completed a little before the

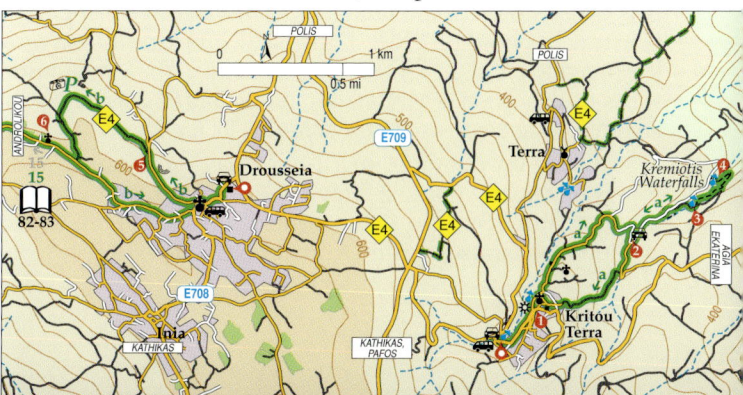

Top: the Byzantine church of Agia Ekaterina lies not far from Kritou Terra. Since this medieval church is more complete than many on Cyprus and contains some faded wall paintings, it is well worth a short (5km) detour during Car tour 1. To reach it, take the crudely signposted road from Kritou Terra (see map — not the Terra road). The church can also be reached within 2km from the Pafos–Polis road at a marked turn-off 1km south of Skoulli.
Left: these beautiful springs in nearby Terra were a communal gathering place.

pandemic, and the reason for the instagram hits. It leads to what many think is the most beautiful waterfall in Cyprus — so lush and green is the moss-coating here that you might think yourself in Bali. You can choose to get there via the 'hole' hewn in the rock by a farmer who wanted to divert water to his fields. But you can also use the new bridge to access the LOWER AND MORE IMPRESSIVE **Kremiotis Waterfall** (❹; **50min**), where there is only room for about five people at time (hence the queues).

Return the same way to the car park (❷), then keep straight ahead on a different track, back to **Kritou Terra** (○; **1h45min**).

Start Walk b at the car park behind the hotel (○). Walk up into the village, passing Finikas Taverna. Turn right between two coffee houses, descending above the OPEN-AIR THEATRE. Go straight ahead on Odos Karis (signed in Greek) and turn left on concrete at an E4 arrow (❺; **15min**). You get fantastic views of the Troodos Mountains and the north coast and pass an interesting ROCK OUTCROP (**25min**; Picnic 22b).

Carry on via vineyards, to a T-JUNCTION (❻; **30min**). Your way is to the left, but first walk a short way to the right (the route of Walk 15) — to a tiny MODERN CHURCH. Then return and, now on tarmac, regain **Drousseia** (○; **1h**).

Walk 23: MILIOU • THELETRA • MILIOU

Distance: 10.5km/6.5mi; 2h55min
Grade: ● strenuous, with steep ascents/descents (300m/1000ft overall). All tracks are good, if muddy after rain. The *multiplicity* of tracks can lead to doubts, but the map is precise.
Equipment: walking boots or stout shoes, sunhat, picnic, water; trekking poles useful
Transport: 🚗 to/from Miliou, a detour from the 83km-point on Car tour 1. Shortly before Miliou, pass the Agii Anargyri Hotel, then park in a small lay-by just after crossing a bridge with iron railings (34° 56.200'N, 32° 27.871'E). (Bus times from Polis are inconvenient.)

Short walk: Miliou views (2.5km/1.6mi; 45min; ● easy, with an ascent/descent of only 60m/200ft). Follow the main walk to the SMALL JUNCTION (**❸**; 25min), enjoy the splendid views, and return the same way.

This is a glorious hike with far-reaching views, sometimes over the whole walk route. The deserted village of Kato Theletra is fascinating to explore and provides a welcome shady pause before the second leg of the walk. *Be sure to follow the instructions carefully* — the whole area is cultivated and covered with a myriad of tracks.

Start the walk at the LAY-BY in **Miliou** (**O**): head back the way you came, up past the AGII ANARGYRI HOTEL. Notice the high ridge to the right, overlooking the valley. The return route runs along the ridge, a little below the top. Look out also for resident peregrine falcons, easily identified by their alternate flapping and gliding.

As the road bends sharp left go straight ahead on a concrete track (**❶**; **8min**). At a Y-FORK (**❷**) 200m from the road, old Kato Theletra is visible in the distance, with the church of new Pano Theletra perched above it — and the whole walk is laid out before you. Go right here and descend the concrete track into the **Neradhes Valley**. Cross the watercourse ('Stream of the Fairies'; **14min**), then bear right and start climbing, ignoring tracks left and right. Some 350m/yds up from the watercourse (**21min**), on an uphill bend to the right, take the lesser track off left — *that is, keeping straight on*. Continue for 200m up to a SMALL JUNCTION (**❸**; **25min**). To the left are panoramic views across groves to the hills, with the village of Yiolou just visible on the ridge (Picnic 23). *(The Short walk turns back here.)*

Continue straight ahead on the main route and within about 275m, at a Y-fork (where the track you are on bends left, back towards the Neradhes Valley), go uphill to the right (**29min**), passing a Wildlife Conservation Area sign on the left. Ignore a clear track off left after 70m. At a Y-fork after a further 200m (on crossing a small gully), stay left, and soon start to descend towards the Neradhes Gorge. Keep left at the next Y-fork (**36min**), and ignore a track running sharply back to the left 90m further on, as you head down between almond groves and vineyards. A LARGE HOUSE across the valley on your left confirms your route. Cross a narrow ravine (**44min**) and, at the next Y-fork, go left downhill. Follow the main track as it crosses the fertile **Neradhes** streambed, lined with giant reeds (**48min**). Go straight on at a junction, following the streambed. This damp area, where there is sometimes a sizeable pool, attracts birds. At a fork, go uphill to the left and undulate gently alongside the stream, eventually crossing it again. The track (sometimes concreted) then zigzags steeply uphill, passing a CHAPEL on the left. *Be sure to take the sharp left uphill track at a hairpin bend* (❹; **56min**). Pause often to admire the surroundings and catch your breath.

The track levels out a bit and you reach an asphalt road. The ongoing walk turns up sharp right here, but you will surely wish to explore **Kato Theletra** to the left (❺; **1h09min**). Most houses are still deserted, but some are being restored and there are often locals around, tending the vines and other fruit trees.

Then continue the walk uphill on a wide asphalt road, marvelling at the extent of the Troodos Mountains across the valley. Where the ROAD BENDS SHARP LEFT (❻; **1h18min**), leave it on a concrete downhill track straight ahead (by electricity pole L3-36-21-8). The track reverts to dirt and follows the gorge, passing a deserted smallholding. Ignore all tracks off left and right to groves and the like. At **1h25min** the main track makes a U-bend to the right around the head of the gorge; follow it as it heads briefly eastwards and climbs a concrete section. Go right at a Y-fork 160m from the U-bend, opposite the smallholding passed earlier (on the far side of the valley).

Follow the main track, sometimes concreted, past a track going down right to a rocky outcrop. As you now contour around the slopes you'll see the village of Yiolou over to the right, backed by Mount Olympos. On reaching a SMALL OPEN AREA, ignore the track going back sharp right, and after just a few metres FORK LEFT UPHILL (❼; **1h40min**). Ignore minor tracks and follow the main track to another Y-fork after 100m. Bear right here. Contour round fertile terracing, past vineyards on the left (being replanted when last seen).

As the track you left earlier joins from the left, continue down a rather rough, stony track (**1h49min**). Cross a dip and rise steeply to a MULTIPLE JUNCTION (❽; **2h05min**). Ignore the track off 90° left; take the concreted downhill track straight ahead, with a telegraph pole on your left. Miliou is below to the right. Continue downhill on a sometimes concreted, sometimes stony track. As it bends slightly right, notice a STONE HUT on your left, just before a small crossroads. Continue straight ahead at the crossroads here, following the track down towards a couple of small concrete ELECTRICITY PLANTS next to a telegraph pole. The track winds to the right here, descending gradually round the gorge. A group of concrete WATER TANKS on your left (**2h20min**) confirms your route.

Ten minutes later you arrive at the ASPHALT ROAD (**9**) from Pano Akourdhalia, coming in from the left. Walk down this road to the first houses in **Miliou** (**2h 36min**). You pass the friendly village coffee house/ restaurant off to your left. Continue straight on, winding downhill, out of the village, back to the LAY-BY (**O**; **2h55min**).

Gourds; Kato Theletra

Walk 24: AGIOS GEORGIOS ALAMANOU TO GOVERNOR'S BEACH

Distance: 5-7km/3-4.3mi; 1h30min-2h10min
Grade: 🟢 very easy, but sometimes rough underfoot; *no shade en route*
Equipment: stout shoes, sunhat, water, swimwear
Transport: 🚗 with friends or taxi to Agios Georgios Alamanou (34° 43.213'N, 33° 13.660'E) or to the large parking area at the eponymous beach, south of the monastery (34° 42.449'N, 33° 14.096'E). *To return:* 🚌 95A from Governor's Beach to the Old Port in Lemesos, May 1st to September 30th *only*: departs 16.30. If you leave your own transport at the start, you'll have to take a taxi back.

If Governor's Beach were white or golden in colour, developers would have had their way with it by now. But its grey (though clean) appearance has saved this popular retreat from touristic blandness. No one would include it in a list of the world's great watering-holes, but its informal — even ramshackle — atmosphere makes for a happy finish to this easiest of strolls. The walk can be accomplished with ease in either direction, but hire-car drivers might find it most agreeable to start at the monastery of Agios Georgios Alamanou, walk to Governor's Beach for a swim and lunch, then return. The monastery is not particularly ancient, but its blue and white galleries and courtyard are very pretty, as you can see in the photo opposite.

To **start the walk** at **Agios Georgios Alamanou**, take the road off to the right just back from the MONASTERY CAR PARK (🔴). Since this road can be heavily trafficked in summer, you may prefer to drive down to the car park at AGIOS GEORGIOS BEACH (🔴) to begin; this would save you 2km, or about half an hour. There is a good fish taverna at this beach (closed from early December to end February). Turn left along the beach for a few minutes, then climb briefly onto a track which frays its way along to Governor's Beach, generally hugging the waterline.

The views are best as you approach **Cape Dolos**, where rock shelves jut out into the sea. Either stay on the track here, or first

Governor's Beach

Walk 24: Agios Georgios Alamanou and Governor's Beach 107

The blue and white galleries and courtyard at the monastery of Agios Georgios Alamanou: the sisters here sell flowers, jam, eggs and chickens, and icons.

rise a bit up the headland road at the Cape (near the Girl Guides' campsite), to survey the scene around **Governor's Beach** (❷) and then descend to the signposted tavernas. Your journey from the monastery should take about **1h45min**. From the beach walk inland to the BUS STOP (❸) below Governor's Beach Camping if you're visiting between May and September. Or call for a taxi, if the effort of lunch has been too much!

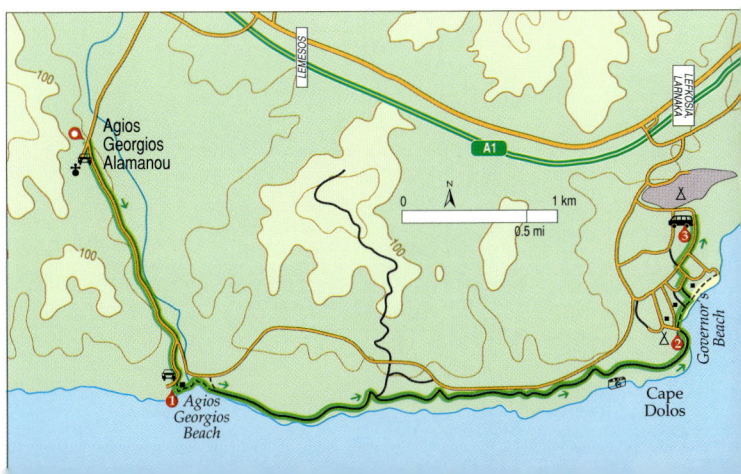

Walk 25: FROM KELLAKI TO PHINIKARIA

Distance: 12km/7.4mi; 3h
Grade: ●! moderate; you should be sure-footed and have a head for heights. Ascents of 150m/490ft; descent of 550m/1800ft overall
Equipment: stout shoes or boots, sunhat, water, picnic
Transport: 🚌 to Kellaki (Timetable B11); alight 1.6km south of the village, at the junction with the road to Prastio. *To return:* 🚌 from Phinikaria to Lemesos (Timetable B10)

Short walk: Phinikaria Fisherman's Trail (1.5km/0.9mi; 30min or more; ● easy, trainers will suffice). Drive across the wall of Germasogia Dam and on to the signposted nature trail: as you enter Phinikaria turn left on a small road which skirts the very edge of the reservoir until you come to a small car park on your left where the road bends uphill to the right (**ⓐ**; 34° 45.394'N, 33° 5.774'E). Walk down from the car park to an INFORMATION BOARD and map. It takes about 30 minutes to walk the circuit around the peninsula (a little over 1km), but it is also worth climbing the steps to the SHELTER on the central hill (**ⓑ**; Picnic 25a).

Alternative circuits for motorists

1 Circuit below Kyparissia (8km/5mi; 2h25min; ●! moderate, with ascents/descents of 300m/985ft overall; you should be sure-footed and have a head for heights). 🚗 Drive to the junction at the start of the main walk and, following instructions for the main walk, drive along the road, then forest road, for about 2km, to **❷**. Park here neatly (34° 47.701'N, 33° 8.194'E) and follow the notes for the main walk from the 31min-point to the 1h26min-point at **❺**

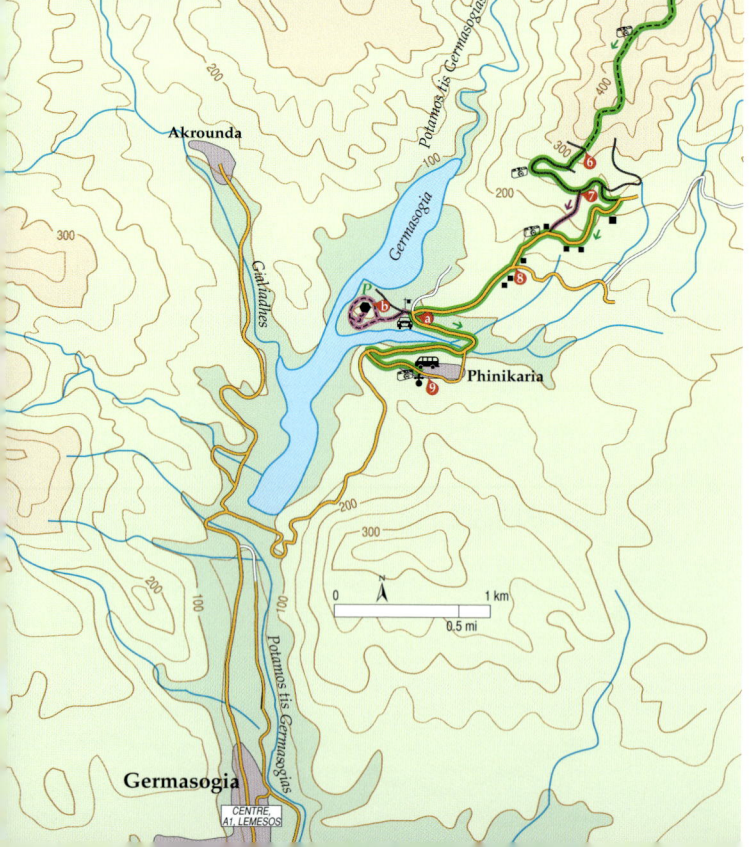

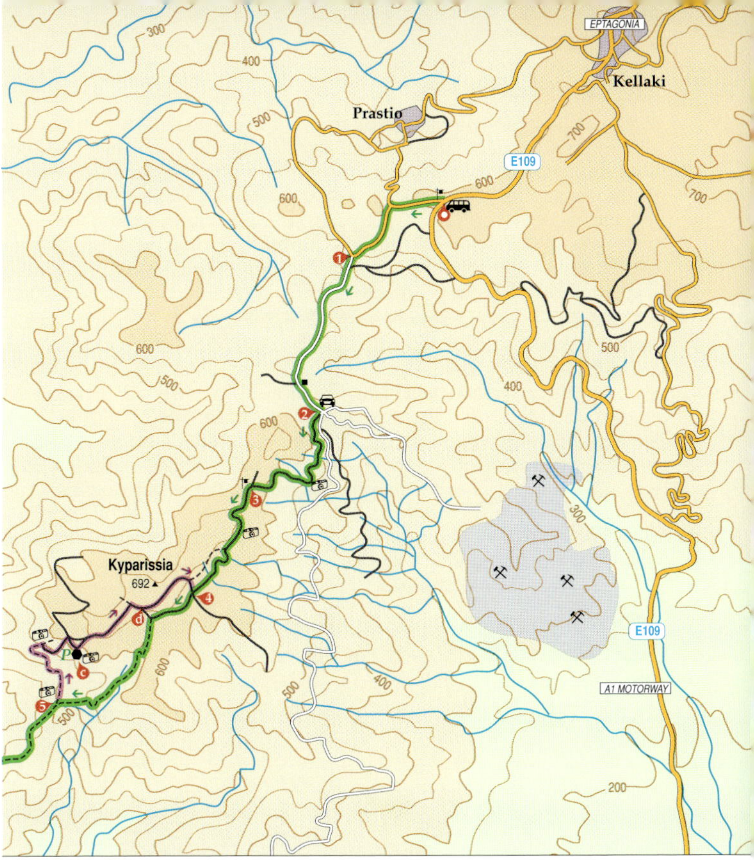

(55min). Turn sharp right uphill and climb through thinning pines. Wind round the slopes, rising gradually with ever-changing views. Pass a bench just after a sharp right turn and almost immediately come to a junction. Turn sharp right here; a rocky track takes you steeply up to a fork. Go right and reach a

Kellaki

secondary peak of Kyparissia, where there is a wooden SHELTER with views in all directions (**c**; 1h23min, Picnic 25b) — a matchless panorama — from Mount Olympos in the north to the dam in the south, Kouklia in the west and the mountains above Larnaka in the east. Continue downhill on this track, walking under the MAIN PEAK of **Kyparissia**. You will reach a bench where the track forks (**d**). Take the left fork, to complete the loop at the 4-way junction (**4**; 1h40min). Then take the wide track of your outward route, to return to your car at **2** (2h25min).

2 Circuit from Germasogia Dam (12.7km/7.9mi; 4h; ●❗ quite strenuous,

with an ascent/descent of 620m/2035ft). You should be sure-footed and have a head for heights. Although most of this walk is out and back, it is a brilliant hike, much of it on mountain paths — a proper hikers' day out. Drive to the CAR PARK for the Short walk on page 103 (**a**; 34° 45.394'N, 33° 5.774'E). Walk up the asphalt road opposite (Lapithou Street) and after 12 minutes turn off left on Kyparissouvouno Street (**8**; there may be a green hikers sign). This is the 2h33min-point of the main walk; referring to the map, follow the main walk in reverse from **8** back to its 1h26min-point (**5**; the path off left below Kyparissia, marked by a hikers' sign) and then pick up the notes for *Alternative walk 1*. When you reach the 4-way junction (**4**), pick up the main walk again at the 1h-point and follow it back to your car at **a** (4h).

On this walk you'll pass from rugged mountainside to gentle countryside enjoying the varied scenery — a deep gorge, a vast (but perhaps dry) dam and splendid views. On the heights there are plenty of kestrels and partridges; lower down, the mixed vegetation, water and nearby houses make a fine habitat

Walk 25: From Kellaki to Phinikaria

for small birds like coal tits, goldfinches, blackcaps and Sardinian warblers.

Start the walk on the E109 road at the JUNCTION SIGNPOSTED TO PRASTIO (**0**), 1.6km south of Kellaki. Follow the road downhill for 350m/yds, ignoring the right turn to Prastio. Continue on road for another 400m/yds, then turn left (due south) on a forestry road where there is a signpost 'KYPARISSIA TRAIL 2.5KM' (**1**). Ignore all turn-offs and keep on this motorable track, eventually passing a little house on the left and coming to a major junction of forestry tracks (just under 2km; **2**; **31min**). Fork right, uphill, here. *(Alternative walk 1 drives to this point and joins the main walk.)* You are now climbing on a steep rough track with sheer drops down left into the valley. Pause to take in the magnificent views.

Reach a junction with signs and a bench, the official start of the **Kyparissia Trail** (**3**; **45min**). Follow the trail and the GREEN HIKERS SIGN left past the information board and walk sharp left uphill. You'll almost feel you are climbing to the stars! But the way soon levels out (**55min**) and brings you to a 4-WAY JUNCTION, also with a bench (**4**; **1h**). Follow the arrow pointing downhill, almost straight ahead. You pass a track joining from the right as your track becomes a path and descends more steadily. Notice the first of the very few tree identification signs on the left and then look up to the right to see the hexagonal shelter visited on Alternative walk 1 (**1h14min**; Picnic 25b). After a few short zigzags walk alongside a stream bed, then cross it (**1h21min**). Continue alongside the stream and after a short rise notice a narrow path going back up to the right, indicated by a GREEN HIKERS

Aerial view over the Germasogia Dam, looking north, with the bridge over the road to Akrounda on the left. But whether you see the dam full of water is anybody's guess — it was bone dry for a couple of years before publication of the last edition, and water had to be shipped in from mainland Greece. But in January 2019 the dam overflowed…

SIGN (**5**; **1h26min**). *(Alternative walk 1 takes this path.)* Continue ahead.

The path begins to descend more sharply and becomes more rocky. You'll soon catch your first views of the **Kyparissia Gorge** (the northerly arm of the Germasogia River) to the right. Wind down through pines and pause to look down to the dam and all the way past Lemesos to the Akrotiri Peninsula (**1h37min**). The path continues to descend and switches to the left side of the ridge for a while, but then back to the right as it descends to meet a track where two HIKERS SIGNS point back the way you have come (**6**; **1h56min**). Turn left, downhill.

Get closer views of the dam and reservoir and in a few minutes pass a track coming in from the left. You will then find yourself heading east, away from the dam, as you begin a long zigzag. But don't worry, you'll soon change direction again as you follow this wide track. You pass a track signed 'PHINIKARIA 3KM' (**7**; **2h10min**) heading down to the right — an optional SHORT-CUT which rejoins the walk at the 2h25min-point, but note that it's steep and can be slippery underfoot. Keeping to the longer track, ignore another track heading left uphill on a hairpin bend (**2h15min**) and continue downhill on the main track, to a T-JUNCTION WITH AN ASPHALT ROAD. Turn right here, keeping a long wooden fence on your left as you walk past an enormous pink villa. At **2h25min** you pass a rough track to the right — the end of the short-cut route.

You now pass fruit groves and a large patch of prickly pears, then reach a T-JUNCTION with another road (**8**; **2h33min**). Turn right and continue to descend towards the dam. There are a few houses by the side of this road, each with superb views … when there is water in the dam. As you round a left hand bend, with a dirt road joining from the right, notice a NATURE TRAIL CAR PARK opposite (●; **2h45min**, Picnic 25a). *This is the starting point for the Short walk.*

Continue left around the bend. After a U-bend to the right, let yourself be tempted by a sign inviting you to head up left to the café in **Phinikaria** (**9**; **3h**) — where the beer and the views are thoroughly recommended (unfortunately it's closed on Mondays). Afterwards, catch a Line 13 bus at the stop opposite for your return to Limassol.

Of course it's possible to walk on to Germasogia: continue down this road, *watching out for local traffic*. You would cross the dam wall after about an hour. Some 350m further on you can turn off left on a gravel track (the old road) beside the river. It soon becomes asphalted; under 2km further on, take a road up to the right, to the main road. Turn left to the main square, where buses leave from opposite the café (about 5h).

Walk 26: MOUNT MAKHERAS

Distance: 5km/3mi; 1h30min
Grade: ● moderate, with an ascent/descent of under 200m/650ft overall
Equipment: stout shoes, sunhat, water, picnic

Bell-tower at Makheras Monastery

114 Landscapes of Cyprus

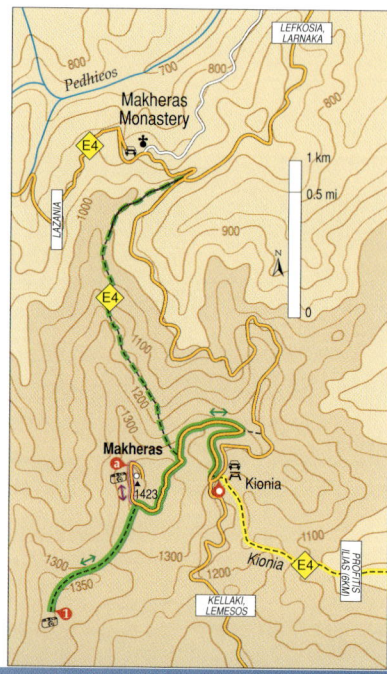

Transport: 🚗 to the Kionia picnic site (34° 55.255'N, 33° 11.861'E). Drive from Lemesos via Kellaki and Agii Vavatsinias; from Larnaka via Kalokhorio, Sha, Mathiati and Kataliondas; from Lefkosia via Analiondas.

Tip: The Kionia Nature Trail to Profitis Ilias Monastery is signposted on the other side of the road. The 7km-long trail runs mostly downhill to the monastery (shown on the touring map), with a climb of some 350m/1150ft on the return (14km/87mi return; 5h). The first kilometre of the path is shown on the map and highlighted in yellow.

This journey to the Makheras Forest in the centre of Cyprus affords a stunning view in all directions after a

Makheras Monastery, second in importance only to Kykko, was founded in 1148, but burned down in 1530 and again in 1892. Most of what the visitor sees today dates from 1900, but the monastery is a very peaceful and beautiful retreat, especially when the almond trees blossom in February. Views from its terraces are quite impressive. In the 1950s, the EOKA organisation had a hide-out in a nearby cave, where second-in-command Gregoris Afxentiou died after a skirmish with British troops. The monastery, like Kykko, has a wealth of icons — including the one said to have inspired its founding. Photo: the monastery at sunset

short uphill walk and an energetic scramble along an easy ridge. As one approaches Mount Makheras, from whatever direction, one becomes increasingly aware of the radar weather station on its summit, perched like a huge golf ball on a giant tee.

Below the peak, which is a few kilometres south of Makheras Monastery, we **begin the walk** at the **Kionia** PICNIC SITE (⬤), with tables, benches, and barbecue facilities. From the site take steps and then a track up to the main road to the summit and follow it uphill. There is no reason why you should not go all the way to the top for the magnificent panorama seen from just outside the gates to the RADAR STATION (⬤).

But the main walk continues from a point on the left of the road, less than 200m/yds below the gates (near a gnarled tree), where you climb over the roadside barrier and scramble briefly down the bank, to head for the obvious ridge. Seen from the tree, the scramble looks easier than it is, but it is not difficult for fit and sure-footed walkers.

After some **30min** come to a first CAIRN and, 500m/yds beyond that, another CAIRN (❶; **45min**) — a beautiful high place where one feels as if all Cyprus is spread below you.

Retrace your steps to the **Kionia** PICNIC SITE (⬤; **1h30min**), and perhaps call at Makheras Monastery, where there is a seasonal café.

Walk 27: STAVROVOUNI MONASTERY

Distance: 4.7km/2.9mi; 1h35min

Grade: ● moderate but steep, sometimes skiddy ascent/descent of 300m/1000ft on a sometimes-overgrown path; *avoid in wet weather.* **No shade**

Equipment: stout shoes, sunhat, water, picnic, long trousers; optional trekking pole(s)

Transport: 🚗 car or taxi to Stavrovouni (a reasonable taxi journey from Larnaka if sharing). Park/alight at the E4 info board (34° 53.731'N, 33° 25.605'E; see below, paragraph 3). Or Lemesos–Lefkosia 🚌 (Timetable A5) to/from the Stavrovouni turn-off (add 5km/3mi overall).

Special note: Men must wear long trousers to enter Stavrovouni or Agia Varvara, and women are not allowed inside either monastery, nor is photography permitted, but the views from the car park are still superb.

For no other reason than to experience the sheer magnificence of the views from the top, the ascent to Stavrovouni, whether on foot or the easy way, is a must for anyone visiting Cyprus. A grand sweep of the eyes round all points of the compass takes in distant mountains, a whole spectrum of landscape colours and dozens of villages and vineyards.

On three sides, Stavrovouni ('Mountain of the Holy Cross') is almost sheer, but the fourth side is negotiable by the sturdy of foot. Approach is via the old Lefkosia–Lemesos road, or a turn-off from the A1 motorway. The last few miles are hardly a delight, distinguished by a stone-crushing plant and the high-profile presence of an army camp. 'No photography' signs abound. But once this is all behind you, the magic begins.

By vehicle or on foot, head first for the smaller monastery of **Agia Varvara** (bee-keeping and icon-painting) and a point 150m/yds beyond it, by an E4 INFO BOARD on the left (○). Then **start the walk** by following the E4 to the top of a rise and looking carefully for the next E4 SIGN (❶; **1min**) — slightly to your left. The path heads down into a gully, then climbs to a wide dirt track. Turn right here, walk along the track for a few metres/yards, then pick up the E4 PATH (❷; **4min**) again on your left. It crosses another track and starts to climb the hillside.

All you have to do now is climb steadily to heaven! The way is sometimes steep but follows a clear path — and there are log steps to help you up the most difficult sections. (The path has been redesigned in the last few years, zigzagging up the contours to make the ascent less brutal than it was in the past.) When your path touches on the hairpin bends of the motor road, look for the E4 signs to continue on the trail.

Your reward, from the top at **Stavrovouni Monastery** (688m/2250ft; ❸; **50min**), is the finest panorama on Cyprus (Picnic 27). The monastery itself is worth looking at, but it should be noted that women visitors are not allowed inside. Stavrovouni is regarded as the oldest monastery on Cyprus,

Walk 27: Stavrovouni Monastery 117

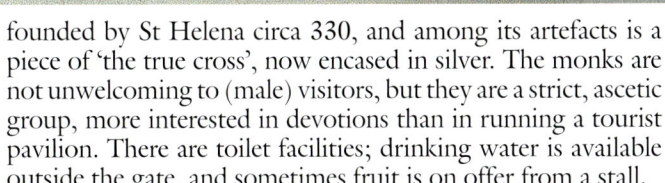

founded by St Helena circa 330, and among its artefacts is a piece of 'the true cross', now encased in silver. The monks are not unwelcoming to (male) visitors, but they are a strict, ascetic group, more interested in devotions than in running a tourist pavilion. There are toilet facilities; drinking water is available outside the gate, and sometimes fruit is on offer from a stall.

The way back down is a choice of either retracing one's footsteps or walking down the motor road. You should be back at the E4 INFO BOARD (⭕) at around **1h35min**, but more if you linger at the top ... and who would not?

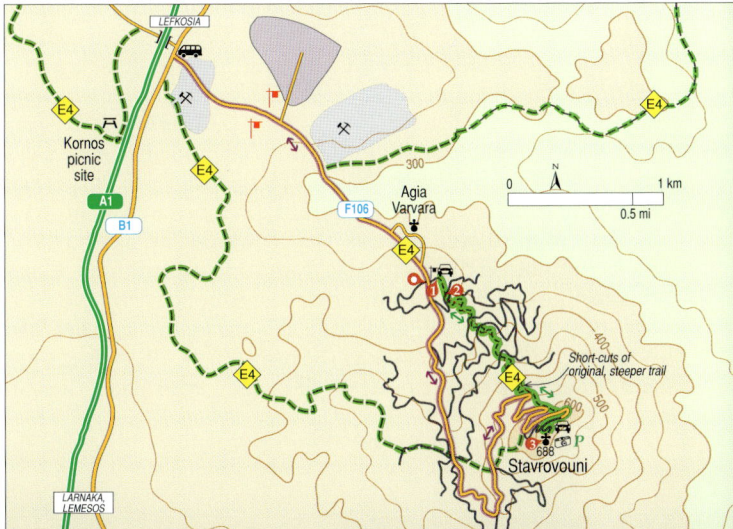

Walk 28: AROUND CAPE KITI

Distance: 11.5km/7.1mi; 3h

Grade: ● easy, level walking, mostly on lanes and tracks, some stretches along the pebbly beach. *No shade, best done from November to April*

Equipment: stout shoes, sunhat, water, picnic, bathing things

Transport: 🚌 to Kiti (Car tour 6). On entering Kiti from the Larnaka direction do *not* turn right towards the famous Panagia Angeloktistos church. Instead continue into the village centre and look for the other, tiny, church in the village square. Park in the car park directly opposite (34° 50.633'N, 33° 34.442'E). Or 🚐 to/from Kiti (Timetable C8).

Shorter circuit: **Agios Leonidos and Kiti Tower from the lighthouse** (8km/ 5mi; 2h15min; ● easy). Access by 🚌 to Kiti lighthouse ('Faros'; ❸; 34° 49.028'N, 33° 36.157'E). Follow the main walk from ❸ (the 1h26min-point) to ❼ (the 2h28min-point). Go straight on (right), heading south towards the lighthouse. After just over 350m/yds turn left on a road signposted to Larnaka; you'll see the watchtower ahead. The road runs between fields. Join the main walk at ❶ (the 35min-point), as it comes in from the left, and follow it back to the lighthouse (❸; 2h15min). There is also a 🚐 to Perivolia (Timetable C9).

Panagia Angeloktistos ('built by angels') is a must for visitors to the Larnaka area. So before setting off, be sure to admire the beautiful mosaic of the Virgin Mary in the apse. This walk is for those who enjoy taking in the ambience of Cyprus through a gentle stroll. In truth it is a long stroll, but is basically flat. Features are a Venetian watchtower, a lighthouse and a charismatic church with an interesting cemetery. In addition you will see many tourists, expatriates and Cypriots, at leisure, and you may surprise some of them on the beach in less than formal attire!

Start the walk in **Kiti**, at the CAR PARK (○) opposite the tiny CHURCH in the market square. Ignore the F406 road signed to the lighthouse and Perivolia, instead walk out of town down SYNERGASIAS STREET (from the southeast corner of the square), passing the TOWN CLINIC (KOINOTIKO IATPEIO) on your right. After 400m/yds turn right towards 'PERIVOLIA'; then, after just 40m/yds, take the first left onto a country road. The watchtower, which is your first objective, is visible directly ahead above the trees. With cultivated fields all around, cross another road, heading slightly to the left (**25min**). After crossing another road, you reach a T-JUNCTION (❶; **35min**). *(The Short walk comes in from the right here.)* Turn left, and after 300m/yds turn right. Take the second track off left, 350m/yds further on, to rise up to **Kiti Tower** (❷; **48min**), a Venetian watchtower.

Admire the tower and the views towards Larnaka Bay, and then continue on the motorable track to an asphalt road. Cross this and, going slightly right, enter a large holiday complex. Go between the rows of villas directly ahead on a pedestrian walkway, to get to the BEACH (**56min**; Picnic 28). Turn right and either walk on the beach itself or the 'promenade' (just an

Walk 28: Around Cape Kiti

Right: the beautifully-kept church and cemetery of Agios Leonidos outside Perivolia. Below: Kiti Tower, dating from the 15th century, is fenced off — making photography difficult.

unmade road), with fields on the right. On approaching another resort you will have to use the beach, now sandy but compact, until you reach the LIGHTHOUSE (**3**; **1h26min**).

Continue round the headland on the pebbly beach. (Or, if the sea is high, take one of the uphill paths cutting across the headland by walking a short distance past the lighthouse and a taverna; then, when you reach a white statue at the entrance to a municipal park, turn left past the swings and follow the path back to the beach to continue.)

Some of the new seafront developments here have gardens which reach almost to the sea, so you may have to dodge the

waves from time to time! As the seaside villas start to thin out, look for two villas, each with SMALL JETTIES (**4**; **2h**). Turn inland between these villas and walk a few metres across open ground, then turn left on SPATHARIKOU STREET. After a few metres, turn right on PAVLOU KOUNDOURGIOTI. Follow this road past some houses and open fields to a crossroads (**2h13min**). You have been able to see a church for some time, and you are now heading straight for it — perhaps guided by bee-eaters and a red kite. Cross this road and take another road towards the church, eventually turning left on a track. Beautifully maintained **Agios Leonidos** (**5**; **2h19min**) is a tranquil resting place.

When you have wandered around and enjoyed this setting, continue on the road past the CEMETERY, signed to LARNAKA. Keep straight on and, just past **Agia Irini** (**6**) on the left, turn left on 'taverna street' (the F406) in **Perivolia** (**7**; **2h28min**). *(The Short walk ignores the delights of the tavernas and continues ahead here.)* At the end of the 100m-long pedestrianised zone devoted to the pleasures of the table, turn right and continue ahead for just under 600m/yds, to a crossroads (**2h38min**). Turn left on ANISTAFIOS AVENUE and follow this suburban street through houses. After another 600m turn left on CHRISTOFOROUS PAPANIKOLOU; then, 500m further on, right on ELLADUS STREET. Pass the road you took to Kiti Tower on your right and, at the T-junction 40m ahead, turn left, retracing your steps to the CAR PARK and tiny CHURCH in **Kiti** (**0**; **3h**).

Panagia Angeloktistos

Walk 29: AGIA NAPA • CAPE GRECO • PROTARAS

Distance: 15km/9.3mi; 4h
Grade: ● quite easy, but with tricky stretches over razor-sharp rocks
Equipment: boots (*ankle protection is essential in the latter part of the walk*), sunhat, water, picnic, swimming things
Transport: 🚌 to Agia Napa (Timetables A7, C7). Local buses also serve the Agia Napa/Protaras/Paralimni area (Timetables D6, D7; re-check times at a tourist office). *To return:* 🚌 local Agia Napa/Protaras/Paralimni (Timetables D6, D7). *Users have warned of doing the walk in reverse: the buses from Agia Napa to Protaras are usually full from midday onwards.*
Short walk: This walk can be shortened at almost any point by reaching the coast road and flagging down a bus, or calling for a taxi from any of the hotels. Stout shoes will suffice as far as Kermia Beach.

The far reaches of any island always hold fascination for the traveller, and this southeastern corner of Cyprus is no exception. It is easily accessible too — Agia Napa is one of the island's most popular tourist centres. This walk takes in sandy beaches, quiet coves, a radar-topped headland and an attractively-sited church.

Begin the walk on LEOFOROS KRYOU NEROU in **Agia Napa**, just north of the GRECIAN SANDS HOTEL (**O**). Joining the E4, take the crazy-paved track just east of the hotel sign that leads seawards, offering a pleasing view over Agia Napa beach within two minutes. Then simply keep close to the sea and head eastwards, experiencing a palm-planted 'promenade' (Picnic 29), little sandy beaches, rocky inlets and, at about **40min**, **Kermia Beach** (**❶**) and its apartments.

A few minutes beyond here, the promenade ends and the going gets tricky if you want to keep to the coast, rather than follow the inland path. It is not difficult to pick a way through the sharp-edged rocks underfoot, but great care should be taken to avoid ankle injury. Progress here will be slower, but you will have a fine view of inlets where waves crash into sea caves (see page 124).

At around **1h15min**, perhaps sooner, you will approach the dominant HEADLAND which has been in view throughout the walk (but it's not Cape Greco!). Better here to move away from the sea, and join the track ahead to the left. A worthwhile detour at this point is to enjoy one of the FORESTRY DEPARTMENT NATURE TRAILS (**❸**) on this headland, now incorporated into the E4 (highlighted on our map with dashed green lines); you'll have splendid views over Cape Greco and along to Agia Napa. From the top of this flat headland (93m) one can even pick out Stavrovouni (Walk 27) in the west and — on very clear days — see the mountains on the far side of the Med. It's just 1km by track from the top to the main road, where you could catch a bus and end the walk.

122　Landscapes of Cyprus

If you are pressing on to Cape Greco, keep to (or rejoin) the route at the base of the headland, round it, then catch a first glimpse of the cape with its lighthouse and the relay masts of Radio Monte Carlo. A little further on, look to a military radar installation high on the left. Following the E4, keep to the right of a cultivated area, climb a low hill, then take a track down to the **Cape Greco** ROAD (❹). You'll have a closer view to the radio masts here, but a locked gate 750m further east prevents access to the lighthouse.

Walk 29: Agia Napa • Cape Greco • Protaras 123

Cross the road and make for the eastern side of the cape, where you'll find the picturesque little church of **Agii Anargyri** (**5**; **2h**). You could end the walk here, by heading up the road and catching a bus back to Agia Napa on the E307. Otherwise, follow the E4 path off to the right, along the edge of a not-very-high cliff towards a sandy beach visible from the church.

You soon come to a road zigzagging down to sandy **Konnos Bay** (**6**; **2h15min**), but don't follow it down to the beach. Cross a BRIDGE on the left and follow a path overlooking the

Looking back to Agia Napa from the sea caves east of Kermia Beach

beach (there may be a sign for 'Cyclop's Cave here). Beyond another, more rocky bay down to the right, bear left for a moment to observe **Cyclop's Cave** in the hillside (❼; **2h45min**), but return to follow the edge of the cliff. Vertigo is a small risk, but easily avoided. Some miles off the cape there is believed to lie the wreck of a 15th-century Genoese ship, as yet undiscovered.

Beyond the boulders and undergrowth of an old quarry, you come to a broad track heading left past an improvised parking area, but keep seawards for a minute or two, then head left to walk parallel with the shore, about 100m/yds inland. To the left is a villa development, ahead is a WINDMILL (❽), and away to the right a jagged, rocky area leading to the sea. Explore it if you wish, but watch your ankles!

From here, progress is over a completely flat coastal strip. Beyond the windmill, you could head up to the junction of the E306/E307 for a bus, if you're flagging. Otherwise, make your way past a seemingly endless succession of new resorts, over rocks, and round sandy inlets, until it's time to head inland to the main road and bus stops in **Protaras** (❾; **4h**).

Walk 30: AGIA NAPA TO PROFITIS ILIAS

Map on pages 122-123; see also photos on pages 39, 122, 123 and opposite
Distance: 8km/5mi; 2h05min
Grade: 🔵 quite easy; ascent/descent of about 150m/490ft
Equipment: walking boots or stout shoes, sunhat, water, picnic
Transport: 🚌 to Agia Napa (Timetables A7, C7). Local buses also serve the Agia Napa/Protaras/Paralimni area (Timetables D6, D7; re-check times at a tourist office). *To return:* 🚌 local Agia Napa/Protaras/Paralimni (Timetables D6, D7). *Users have warned of doing the walk in reverse: the buses from Agia Napa to Protaras are usually full from midday onwards.*
Short walk: **Agii Saranta** (2km/1.2mi; 45min return; 🟢 easy). 🚗 drive the first part of the walk, along the rough road, and park short of the transmitter (❶; 35° 0.268'N, 34° 1.793'E). Then use the notes below from ❷ (the 35min-point) to ❸ (the 50min-point) and return the same way.
Tip: There is a signposted CTO trail running *inland* between Konnos Bay and Profitis Ilias via Agios Ioannis and Agii Saranta (see yellow highlighting on our map). We pick up this trail just southwest of Agii Saranta and follow it to Profitis Ilias. The E4 uses part of this route.

This walk explores the gentle agricultural hills behind Agia Napa and Protaras. Prise yourself away from the golden beaches and you'll find that some modest exertion reveals a different world… of wind-powered wells, rich red soil producing a harvest of vegetables, quaint little churches, and a few stony tracks waiting to be explored.

The walk can be done in either direction, but it is easier to locate the **start at Agia Napa** (note also the comment above about return buses). From the ROUNDABOUT BY THE MONASTERY (⭕), walk north on the PARALIMNI ROAD, and turn right (with the E4) just past the POLICE STATION on a road that leads in **10min** or less to the community STADIUM (❶). Turn left soon after passing this, and continue round the edge of PLAYING FIELDS. Then take the third road to the right (450m further on and signed to 'Phanos'), heading towards a radio transmitter mast in the middle distance. Some 300m short of the mast, the route (by now a motorable track), makes a definite left turn. At this point, you should TURN OFF RIGHT ON A PATH (❷; **35min**) and then immediately right again. You walk through an area of low trees and come to an open area from where there are views to Cape Greco.

After 400m, the path joins the CTO/E4 trail, a motor track which you follow left, to **Agii Saranta** (❸; **50min**; Picnic 30). This most unusual, tiny church (shown overleaf) is set in a cave, and its only light comes from the dome on the hillside above it. Inside you will find evidence of a latter-day icon painter at work, and the familiar candles.

Continue on the CTO trail beyond Agii Saranta for about 10 minutes (650m), to a fork where 'Panagia' is signposted to the right; keep straight ahead for 'PROFITIS ILIAS' (❹), with the

126 Landscapes of Cyprus

transmitter mast away to the left. At **1h05min** or less you should be getting views off to the right — to the imposing church of Profitis Ilias on its rocky perch, with Protaras behind it. Keep to the track, with the transmitter mast away to the left, and come to a POWER PLANT (**5**). Turn 90° right off the main track here, and follow a faint track towards and then past a cylindrical WATER TANK (**6**). When asphalt comes underfoot at a villa development, keep downhill, then climb the steps to **Profitis Ilias** (**7**; **2h**). Views from the church and its pedestal are pleasing; the church is modern but very attractive inside and out. From Profitis Ilias descend steps to the MAIN COAST ROAD (**8**; **2h05min**) and pick up a bus or taxi.

Agii Saranta

SERVICE TAXI AND BUS TIMETABLES

Below are relevant destinations served by public transport. The number after the place name is the **timetable number**. Timetables follow on the next seven pages, but *do* download the latest timetables for any service you may use just before you travel. You can usually get all the relevant information you need (with interactive maps) at **www.cyprusbybus.com**. But for rural and suburban services, if cyprusbybus.com does not have the timetable, you will have to log on to the individual operators' websites shown for the various areas. Departure points for buses and service taxis are shown on the town plans (see pages 8-13) and the walking maps.

Agia Napa
— Larnaka C7, D1, D3
— Lefkosia A7, D2
— Paralimni D1-D7
Agios Georgios — Pafos E6
Agios Neophytos — Pafos E9
Agros — Lemesos B8
Arkhimandrita — Pafos E10
Baths of Aphrodite — Polis F1
Coral Bay — Pafos E8
Germasogia — Lemesos B10
Governor's Beach — Lemesos B12
Kakopetria — Lefkosia A8
Kellaki — Lemesos B11
Kissonerga — Pafos E7
Kiti — Larnaka C8
Lakki — Polis F1
Larnaka (Larnaca)
all destinations C1-C10
— Agia Napa C7
— Kiti C8
— Lefkosia A1, A4, C1, C4
— Lemesos B2, B6, C2, C5
— Pafos C3, E3
— Paralimni C7
— Perivolia C9
— Protaras C7
— tourist beach C10
Lefkosia (Nicosia)
all destinations A1-A10
— Agia Napa D2
— Kakopetria A8
— Larnaka A1, A4, C1, C4
— Lemesos A2, A5, A12, B1, B4
— Pafos A3, A6, E2
— Paralimni A7, D2
— Platres A8
— Protaras A7, D2
— Troodos A10
Lemesos (Limassol)
all destinations B1-B12
— Agros B8
— Germasogia B10
— Governor's Beach B12
— Kellaki B11

— Larnaka B2, B6, C2, C5
— Lefkosia A2, A5, B1, B4
— Pafos B3, B5, E1, E4
— Phinikaria B11
— Platres and Troodos B7
— Prodhromos B7
Pafos (Paphos)
all destinations E1-E9
— Agios Georgios E6
— Agios Neophytos E9
— Arkhimandrita E10
— Coral Bay E8
— Kissonerga E7
— Larnaka C3, E3
— Lefkosia A3, A6, E2
— Lemesos B3, B5, E1, E4
— Polis E5
— Tala E9
Paralimni
— Agia Napa D1-D7
— Larnaka C7, D1, D3
— Lefkosia A7
— Protaras D1-D7
Petra tou Romiou
— Lemesos B5
— Pafos E4
Phinikaria — Lemesos B11
Pissouri
— Lemesos B5
— Pafos E4
Platres
— Lefkosia A8
— Lemesos B7
Polis
— Baths of Aphrodite F1
— Lakki F1
— Pafos E5
Prodhromos
— Lefkosia A8
— Lemesos B7
Protaras
— Agia Napa D1-D7
— Larnaka C7
— Lefkosia A7
— Paralimni D1-D7
Troodos — Lefkosia A10

Services from LEFKOSIA (Nicosia)
INTERCITY SERVICE TAXIS
Operator: 'Travel & Express' — www.travelexpress.com.cy
Address: Municipal Parking Place Kolokasi (Podokatoro)
Telephone/email: 22-730888/taxi@travelexpress.com.cy

A1	Lefkosia to LARNAKA	*Daily,* every half hour from 06.00 to 18.00 (17.00 Sat/Sun)
A2	Lefkosia to LEMESOS	*as A1 above*
A3	Lefkosia to PAFOS	*as A1 above*

INTERCITY BUS SERVICES
Operator: Intercity Buses — www.intercity-buses.com
Address: Solomos Square
Telephone: 8000 7789 or 24-643493 (but for A7 7777 7755 or 22-468088)

A4	Lefkosia to LARNAKA	*Mon-Fri:* 06.00, 07.30, 08.45, 09.30, 10.30, 13.00, 14.00, 14.30, 16.00, 17.30, 18.30, 20.00 *Sat/Sun:* 08.00, 09.30-11.30 (every hour), 13.00, 16.30, 18.00, 19.30
A5	Lefkosia to LEMESOS	*Mon-Fri:* 06.00, 07.00, 08.30-14.30 (hourly), 16.30, 18.30, 20.30 *Sat/Sun:* 07.00, 08.45, 10.30, 13.00-21.00 (every two hours)
A6	Lefkosia to PAFOS	*Mon-Fri:* 05.00, 08.30, 11.00, 14.30, 18.00; *Sat/Sun:* 08.00, 12.00, 15.00, 18.00
A7	Lefkosia to AGIA NAPA and PARALIMNI	*Mon-Fri:* 08.15, 11.30, 15.00, 17.00 *Sat/Sun:* 09.00, 10.00, 18.30

RURAL AND SUBURBAN BUS SERVICES
Operator: OSEL — www.osel.com.cy *(if website not working, use publictransport.com.cy)*
Address: Solomos Square; return buses leave from main stop in village served
Telephone: 7777 7755 or 22-468088

A8	Lefkosia to PLATRES (Route: Platres—Prodhromos—Pedhoulas)	*Mon-Sat only:* 12.15
	PLATRES to Lefkosia (Route: Pedhoulas—Prodhromos—Platres)	*Mon-Sat only:* 06.00 (does not call at Platres on Saturdays unless reserved in advance)
A9	Lefkosia to KAKOPETRIA	*Mon-Fri:* 06.00, 10.20, 11.30, 13.00, 14.00, 14.30, 15.30, 16.20, 16.45, 17.30, 18.00 *Sat:* 11.30, 13.00, 14.00, 17.30 *Sun:* 08.00, 17.00 *(18.00 in July/August)*
	KAKOPETRIA to Lefkosia	*Mon-Fri:* 05.00, 05.45, 06.10, 06.30, 06.45, 08.00, 13.30, 14.30 *Sat:* 06.00, 06.45, 08.00, 14.30 *Sun:* 06.00, 16.30 *(July and August)*
A10	Lefkosia to TROODOS	*Mon-Fri:* 10.20; *Sat:* 11.30 *From Troodos to Platres:* 15.15
	TROODOS to Lefkosia	*Mon-Sat:* 06.30 *(also 17.00 in July/August)*

Services from LEMESOS (Limassol)

INTERCITY SERVICE TAXIS
Operator: 'Travel & Express' — www.travelexpress.com.cy
Address: Vasileos Pavlou A 47
Telephone/email: 25-877666/taxi@travelexpress.com.cy

B1	Lemesos to LEFKOSIA	*Daily,* every half hour from 06.00 to 18.00 (17.00 Sat/Sun)
B2	Lemesos to LARNAKA	*as B1 above*
B3	Lemesos to PAFOS	*as B1 above*

INTERCITY BUS SERVICES
Operator: Intercity Buses — www.intercity-buses.com
Address: New port
Telephone: 8000 7789 or 24-643493

B4	Lemesos to LEFKOSIA	*Mon-Fri:* 05.30, 06.00, 07.30, 09.00, 10.30-14.30 (every hour), 16.30-20.30 (every two hours) *Sat/Sun:* 07.00, 08.45, 10.30, 13.00-21.00 (every hour), 21.00
B5	Lemesos to PAFOS	*Mon-Fri:* 06.15, 07.30, 09.30, 11.30, 13.00, 15.00, 16.00, 17.30, 19.30, 21.00 *Sat/Sun:* 06.00, 07.45, 11.00, 14.30, 17.30, 21.00
B6	Lemesos to LARNAKA	*Mon-Fri:* 06.00, 08.00, 09.00, 10.30, 11.30, 13.30, 14.30, 16.00, 18.00, 19.30 *Sat/Sun:* 08.30, 10.30, 11.30, 14.00, 16.00, 18.00

RURAL AND SUBURBAN BUS SERVICES
Operator: EMEL — www.limassolbuses.com
Address: EMEL Central Station, 194 Leontiou; return buses leave from main stop in village served
Telephone: 7777 8121

B7	Lemesos to PLATRES and TROODOS	Bus 64, *Daily:* 09.30; 18.00 (Mon-Fri only)
	TROODOS to Lemesos	Bus 64, 08.45 (Mon-Fri only), 15.30
	PLATRES to Lemesos	Bus 64, 07.20, 09.00 (not Sun), 15.45
B8	Lemesos to AGROS	Buses 66, 50, *Mon-Sat:* 07.30, 12.00, 13.30, 16.15, 18.15 *Sun:* 11.00, 17.00
	AGROS to Lemesos	Buses 66, 50, *Mon-Sat:* 06.00, 07.00, 09.00; *Sun:* 09.40, 16.10
B9	Lemesos to AMATHUS (hotel area)	Buses 30, 31; service operates along the the coast road approx. every 15 minutes
	AMATHUS (hotel area) to Lemesos	*as above; service starts at Hotel Meridien*
B10	Lemesos to PHINIKARIA and GERMASOGIA	Bus 13, *Mon-Fri:* 08.00 and approx. hourly until 19.05; Bus 13, *Sat:* 08.00, 09.00, 10.00, 11.00; *Sun:* 09.15, 10.15
	GERMASOGIA to Lemesos	Bus 13, *Mon-Fri:* 08.00 and approx. hourly until 16.30; *Sat:* 14.05, 15.25, 16.45; *Sun:* 15.00, 16.00, 17.00

130 Landscapes of Cyprus

B11	Lemesos to KELLAKI	Bus 80, *Mon-Fri:* 11.50, 13.30; *Sat:* 11.50; *Sun:* 10.10
	KELLAKI to Lemesos	Bus 80, *Mon-Fri:* 15.20; *Sat:* 06.15; *Sun:* 15.20
B12	Lemesos to GOVERNOR'S BEACH	Bus 95A, *Daily:* 10.00
	GOVERNOR'S BEACH to Lemesos	Bus 95A, *Daily:* 16.00

Pafos lighthouse

Services from LARNAKA
INTERCITY SERVICE TAXIS
Operator: 'Travel & Express' — www.travelexpress.com.cy
Address: Corner of Papakyriakou and Marselou streets
Telephone/email: 24-661010/taxi@travelexpress.com.cy

C1	Larnaka to LEFKOSIA	*Daily,* every half hour from 06.00 to 18.00 (17.00 Saturdays and Sundays)
C2	Larnaka to LEMESOS	*As C1 above*
C3	Larnaka to PAFOS	*as C1 above*

INTERCITY BUS SERVICES
Operator: Intercity Buses — www.intercity-buses.com
Address: Phinikoudes Avenue (near the Kimon statue)
Telephone: 7000 7789 or 24-643493

C4	Larnaka to LEFKOSIA	*Mon-Fri:* 06.30, 07.15, 09.30-10.30 (every hour), 11.00, 12.00, 13.00, 14.15, 16.30, 18.30, 19.30 *Sat/Sun:* 06.30, 08.00, 09.00, 10.30, 13.00, 16.00-20.00 (every two hours)
C5	Larnaka to LEMESOS	*Mon-Fri:* 06.00, 08.00, 09.00, 10.30, 11.30, 13.30, 14.30, 16.00, 18.00, 19.30 *Sat/Sun:* 08.30, 10.30, 11.30, 14.00, 16.00, 18.00
	Larnaka to PAFOS — *Service is via Lemesos; see Timetables C5 and B5*	
C6	Larnaka to AGIA NAPA/PROTARAS/PARALIMNI	*Mon-Fri:* 06.00, 07.45, 09.15, 10.00, 11.00, 13.00, 14.30, 16.00, 18.00, 19.30 *Sat/Sun:* 08.00, 10.00, 11.30, 14.30, 16.00, 17.30

RURAL AND SUBURBAN BUS SERVICES
Operator: Osea — www.osea.com.cy
Address: bus stop opposite the police station on Leoforos Archbishop Makarious III; return buses leave from main stop in village served
Telephone: 8000 7744 or 23-819090

C7	Larnaka to AGIA NAPA/PROTARAS/PARALIMNI	Bus 711, *Mon-Fri:* 08.15, 10.30, 11.15, 13.45, 16.30, 18.30 *Sat/Sun:* 10.00, 13.30, 15.30, 18.00
	PARALIMNI/PROTARAS/AGIA NAPA to Larnaka: see Timetable D1	

Operator: Zinonas — www.zinonasbuses.com, but the website is not in English; use cyprusbybus.com. *Kiti is also served by Bus 407.*
Address: Phinikoudes Avenue (near the Kimon statue); return buses leave from main stop in village served
Telephone: 8000 7744 or 24-665598

C8	Larnaka to KITI (Angeloktistos Church)	Bus 419, *Mon-Fri:* 06.20, 07.30, 08.30, 09.15, 10.00, 12.00, 14.00, 15.30, 17.00, 18.30, 20.00 *Sat/Sun:* 11.30, 14.00, 15.30, 17.00, 18.30, 20.00
	KITI to Larnaka	Bus 419, *Mon-Fri:* 05.45, 07.40, 09.15, 10.00, 10.45, 11.15, 12.35, 14.45, 16.15, 17.45, 19.15 *Sat/Sun:* 09.15, 10.45, 12.15, 13.15, 14.45, 16.15

132   Landscapes of Cyprus

C9	Larnaka to PERIVOLIA	as Timetable C8
	PERIVOLIA to Larnaka	as Timetable C8
C10	Larnaka to TOURIST BEACH EAST of Larnaka	Bus 431, *Mon-Fri:* 08.30, 10.00, 12.00, 15.00, 16.00, 18.00 *Sat/Sun:* 08.30, 10.00, 12.00, 14.30, 15.30
	TOURIST BEACH EAST to Larnaka	Bus 431, *Mon-Fri:* 08.00, 09.30, 11.30, 14.30, 15.30, 17.30 *Sat/Sun:* 08.00, 09.30, 11.30, 14.00, 15.00, 16.00

Services from AGIA NAPA, PARALIMNI, PROTARAS

INTERCITY SERVICE TAXIS
Operator: 'Travel & Express' — www.travelexpress.com.cy
Address: Griva Digeni 105
Telephone/email: 23-826061/taxi@travelexpress.com.cy

D1	Paralimni to LEFKOSIA	*Daily,* every half hour from 06.00 to 18.00 (17.00 Saturdays and Sundays)
D2	Paralimni to LEMESOS	as D1 above
D3	Paralimni to PAFOS	as D1 above

INTERCITY BUS SERVICES
Operator: Intercity Buses — www.intercity-buses.com
Address: St George in Paralimni; Cape Greco Ave., below Profitis Ilias in Protaras, monastery in Agia Napa
Telephone: 7000 7789 or 24-643493

D4	Paralimni/Protaras/ Agia Napa to LARNACA	*Mon-Fri:* 06.00, 07.45, 08.45, 09.30, 10.45, 14.15, 16.00, 17.30, 19.00, 20.30 *Sat/Sun:* 08.00, 10.00, 11.30, 13.00, 14.30, 16.15, 18.30, 20.00
D5	Paralimni and Agia Napa to LEFKOSIA	*Mon-Fri:* 08.00, 10.30, 13.30, 18.30 *Sat/Sun:* 08.00, 10.00, 17.30, 20.30

D5 Buses leave from St George in Paralimni and the monastery in Agia Napa; for information call 7777 7755 or 22-468088

RURAL AND SUBURBAN BUS SERVICES
Operator: Osea — www.osea.com.cy
Address: in Paralimni: Kappari Avenue (Paralimni); Cape Greco Ave, below Profitis Ilias (Protaras); Corner Makariou/Evangelou Floraki (Agia Napa); return buses leave from main stop in village served
Telephone: 8000 7744 or 23-819090

D6	Paralimni/Protaras/ Agia Napa to LARNAKA	Bus 711, *Mon-Fri:* 08.00, 08.45, 11.00, 14.10, 16.00 *Sat/Sun:* 07.45, 10.30, 13.15, 15.30
	LARNAKA to Agia Napa: see Timetable C7	
D7	Agia Napa to PARALIMNI (via PROTARAS)	Bus 101, *Mon-Sat:* 09.00, 09.30*, 10.00, 10.30*, 11.30*, 12.00, 13.00, 14.00, 14.45*, 16.00, 16.30*, 17.00, 17.30*, 17.45*, 18.00*, 18.30*, 19.00*, 19.30*, 20.00* *Sun:* 09.00*, 10.00*, 11.00*, 12.00*, 13.00*, 14.00*, 16.00*, 17.00* *May-Oct only

PARALIMNI to
Agia Napa
(via PROTARAS)

Bus 102, *Daily, May-Oct:* 09.00, 09.30*, 10.00, 10.30*, 11.00, 11.30*, 12.00, 13.00, 14.00, 15.00*, 16.00, 16.30*, 17.00, 18.00, 19.00, 20.00*
Nov-Apr, Mon-Sat only: 09.00, 10.00, 11.00, 12.00, 13.00, 14.00, 16.00, 17.00
* Not on Sundays

Services from PAFOS

INTERCITY SERVICE TAXIS
Operator: 'Travel & Express' — www.travelexpress.com.cy
Address: 34 Kiniras
Telephone/email: 7777 7474 or 26-923800/taxi@travelexpress.com.cy

E1	Pafos to LEMESOS	*Daily,* every half hour from 06.00 to 18.00 (17.00 Saturdays and Sundays)
E2	Pafos to LEFKOSIA	— *as Timetable E1*
E3	Pafos to LARNAKA	— *as Timetable E1*

INTERCITY BUS SERVICES
Operator: Intercity Buses — www.intercity-buses.com
Address: Karavella Bus Station
Telephone: 8000 7789 or 26-220887

E4   **Pafos to LEMESOS**   *Mon-Fri:* 06.00, 07.30, 09.00, 10.00, 11.00, 14.30, 15.00, 16.30, 18.00, 19.30
Sat/Sun: 07.30, 09.30, 13.00, 16.30, 19.30

Pafos to LEFKOSIA — *Service via Lemesos; see Timetables E4 and B4*
Pafos to LARNAKA — *Service via Lemesos; see Timetable E4 and B6*

RURAL AND SUBURBAN BUS SERVICES
Operator: OSYPA — www.PafosBuses.com
Address: Karavella Bus Station (E5, E7, E9, E10); Kato Pafos Bus Station (E6, E8); return buses leave from main stop in village served
Telephone: 8000 5588 or 26-934252

E5   **Pafos to POLIS**   Bus 645, *Mon-Fri:* 06.20, 08.00, 09.00, 10.00, 11.00, 12.00, 14.00, 15.00, 16.00, 17.00, 18.00
Sat: 08.00, 09.00, 10.00, 11.00, 13.00, 15.00, 16.00, 18.00
Sun: 10.00, 12.00, 13.00, 14.00, 15.00, 17.00

POLIS to Pafos   Bus 645, *Mon-Fri:* 05.30, 06.30, 08.00, 09.00, 10.00, 11.00, 13.00, 13.45, 15.00, 16.00, 17.00
Sat: 08.00, 09.00, 12.00, 14.00, 15.00, 17.00
Sun: 09.00, 11.00, 12.00, 13.00, 14.00, 16.00

E6   **Pafos to AGIOS GEORGIOS**   *First take Bus 615 to Coral Bay (at least every 15 minutes), then* Bus 616A or 616B from Corallia Beach: 08.30, 09.30, 10.20, 10.30, 11.30, 13.10, 13.30, 14.30, 15.00, 15.30, 16.00, 16.30

134   Landscapes of Cyprus

	AGIOS GEORGIOS to Pafos	*First take Bus 616A or 616B to Coral Bay, then* Bus 615 every hour from 09.00-12.00 and from 14.00-17.00 *daily, April-Nov*
E7	Pafos to KISSONERGA	Bus 607, *Mon-Fri:* 06.00, 08.30, 09.50, 11.40, 16.00, 18.00 *Sat:* 07.40, 11.20, 13.40, 16.20
	KISSONERGA to Pafos	Bus 607, *Mon-Fri:* 10.45, 12.50, 17.00 *Sat:* 14.50, 17.20
E8	Pafos to CORAL BAY	Bus 615, *all year round:* too frequent to list, about every 15 min after 6am until midnight
	CORAL BAY to Pafos	Bus 615, *all year round:* too frequent to list, about every 15 min after 6am until midnight
E9	Pafos to AGIOS NEOPHYTOS	Bus 604, *Mon-Fri:* 06.30, 09.20, 11.10, 14.20, 16.00, 17.40 *Sat:* 08.10, 10.50, 15.00, 17.40
	AGIOS NEOPHYTOS to Pafos	Bus 604, *Mon-Fri:* 07.10, 10.00, 11.50, 15.00, 16.40, 18.20 *Sat:* 08.50, 11.30, 15.40, 18.20
E10	Pafos to PANO ARKHIMANDRITA	Bus 632, *Mon-Sat:* 06.15, 10.00, 14.10 (13.30 on Saturdays)
	PANO ARKHIMANDRITA to Pafos	Bus 632, *Mon-Sat:* 07.40, 10.50, 15.00 (14.20 on Saturdays)

Services from POLIS

RURAL AND SUBURBAN BUS SERVICES

Operator: OSYPA — www.PafosBuses.com
Address: Kyproleontos Street (opposite the tourist office); return buses leave from Lakki harbour or restaurant at the Baths of Aphrodite
Telephone: 8000 5588 or 26-934252

F1	Polis to the BATHS OF APHRODITE and LAKKI	Pafos Bus 622, *Mon-Fri:* 06.00, then every hour from 08.00-12.00 and from 15.00-18.00 *Sat/Sun:* 06.00, 10.00, 11.00, 12.00, 14.00, 15.00, 18.00
	LAKKI and the BATHS OF APHRODITE to Polis	Bus 622, *Mon-Fri:* 06.30, then every hour from 08.30 to 12.30 and 15.30 to 18.30 *Sat/Sun:* 06.30, 10.30, 11.30, 12.30, 14.30, 15.30, 18.30

Index

Geographical entries only are included in this index. For other entries, see Contents, page 3. A page number in *italic type* indicates a map reference; a page number in **bold type** indicates a photograph or drawing. Both of these may be in addition to a text reference on the same page. '*TM*' refers to the large-scale *walking map* on the reverse of the touring map. Transport timetables are given on pages 126 to 134.

Adonis Nature Trail **96-7**, 98, 99, 100, *TM*
Agia Ekaterina (church, near Drousseia) **102**
Agia Mavri *67*, **68**
Agia Napa 18, 39, **41**, 43, 49, 121, *122-3*, **122**, **123**, **124**, 125, 126 *town plan 13*
Agiasma Nature Trail **25**, **76-7**, *77*
Agii Pateres (shrine in Pano Arkhimandrita) 26, 88, **89**, *90*
Agii Saranta (cave church, near Protaras) 18, *122-3*, 125, **126**
Agios Ioannis (church, near Protaras) *122-3*, 125
Agios Georgios (north of Pafos) 22, 24, 80, *82-3*, 84, 85
Agios Georgios (church near Alekhtora) **91**, 92, *193*
Agios Georgios Alamanou (monastery) 36, 106, **107**, *107*
Agios Leonidos (church at Perivolia) *118*, **119**, *119*
Agios Minas (church, near the Smigies picnic area) 24, 100, *TM*
Agios Neophytos (monastery) 25, 74, *75*, **75**
Akamas Peninsula 6, **43**, 44, **80-1**, *82-3*, 84, **86**, **96-7**, 98, 99, *TM*
Akoursos 16, **23**, *78*
Alekhtora 17, 27, *87*, 89, *93*
Almyrolivado (picnic site) *56-57*, 58, **58**
Androlikou 24, 84, 100, *TM*

Aphrodite Nature Trail **96-7**, 98, **99**, 100, *TM*
Aphrodite, Baths of (Loutra Aphroditis) 17, 22, 24, **94**, **95**, 97, 98, 99, *TM*
Aphrodite's Rocks 26-7, **cover**
Arsos 26
Artemis Nature Trail 15, 50, 52, *56-7*
Asinou **35**, 36
Asprokremnos Dam 32
Atichoulli Gorge 31
Avagas Gorge 24, **80-1**, *82-3*, 85, **86**
Cape Arnauti 94, **96-7**, *TM*
Cape Greco 39, **40**, 41, 121, **122**, *122-3*, 125
Cape Kiti 118, **119**, *119*
Cedar Valley 16, 28, 72, **73**, *73*
Chromion 50, 52, *56-7*
Chrysorroyiatissa (monastery) 28, 31
Coral Bay 17, 22, 24, **78**, *79*
Dhekelia 27, 40, 41
Dherinia 39, 40
Dhiarizos Valley **32-3**
Dhodheka Anemi 16, 28, 29, *68*, 72, *73*
Dhora 26, 33
Dhromolaxia 37, 38
Doxasi o Theos Nature Trail **64-5**, *66*
Drousseia 17, 22, 24, 43, *82-3*, 84, *101*, 102
Episkopi 26, 27
Evretou Dam 31
Famagusta 40
Fasli 24
Fig Tree Bay *see* Protaras
Fontana Amorosa 94, 95, 97, *TM*
Galata 34, 36

Germasogia 36, *108-9*, 112
Germasogia Dam *108-9*, **110-1**
Geroskipou 26, 35
Governor's Beach 35, **106**, *107*
Hala Sultan Tekke (mosque) 35, **37**, 38
Horteri Nature Trail 28, *69*, 71
Kakopetria 34, 36, 44, 59
Kaledonia Falls 16, 53, **54**, 55, *56-7*
Kalokhorio 37, 38, 114
Kambi tou Kalogerou (picnic site) *56-7*, 63
Kambos tou Livadiou (picnic site) 16, *56-7*, 58, 59
Kannaviou 28, 31, 69, 73
Kathikas 17, 22, **25**, 44, *76*, *77*
Kato Arkhimandrita 87, **88-9**, *90*, 91
Kato Arodhes 22, **25**
Kato Theltera 23, 25, 103, 104, **105**, *105*
Kedhares 33
Kellaki *108-9*, **109**, 111
Kermia Beach 18, 121, *122-3*, **124**
Khapotami Gorge 17, 27, *87*, 89, 90, 91, 92, *93*
Khoulou 31
Kionia (Nature Trail and picnic site) **114**, 115
Kissonerga 22, 24, 78, 79
Kiti 18, 37, 38, **119**, *119*, **120**
Kiti Tower **119**
Konnos Bay *122-3*
Kophinou 37, 38
Kornos Forestry Station 34, 37, 38
Kouka *67*, **68**
Kouklia 18, 26-7, 32
Kourion 26, 27

135

136 Landscapes of Cyprus

Kremiotis Waterfalls 18, *101*, **102**
Kritou Terra 22, *101*, **102**
Kryos Potamos (river) 15, 16, 53, **54**, *56-7*, 60
Kykko (monastery) 28, **29**, **30-1**, 69, 72, 115
Kyparissia (peak) *108-9*, 110, 111
Kyperounda 16, 36, *64-5*, 66
Lagoudhera *64-5*, **65**
Lakki **4**, 22, 23, 24, 44, 49, 94, 98, *TM*
Lakko tou Frankou **91**, *93*
Laona (area) 22, 23, 76, 85
Lara Beach 6, **14-5**, 17, 24, 80, 81, *82-3*, 84
Larnaka (Larnaca) 35, **37**, 39, 41, 44, 49, 106, 116, 118
town plan 11
Lefkara 36
Lefkosia (Nicosia) 5, 20, 21, 29, 32, 33, 34, 36
town plan 8-9
Lemesos (Limassol) 34, 36, 44, 49, 106, 108
town plan 12-3
Lofou *67*, **68**
Lyso 31, 69, 71
Madhari Ridge 16, *64-5*, **67**
Makheras (monastery) **113**, *114*, **115**
Makrya Kontarka 16, 53, *56-7*
Mallia 33
Mandria 26, 33
Mavrokolymbos Dam 17, 22, *79*, **79**
Mesapotamos (monastery) 16, *56-7*
Miliou 18, 23, 103, 104, *105*
Mount Adelphi 16, *64-5*, **66**
Mount Makheras 113, *114*
Mount Olympos 15, 34, 44, 45, 50, **51**, *56-7*
Mount Tripylos 16, 28, 72, *73*

Moutti tis Sotiras (plateau) 97, 98, 99, *TM*
Neo Chorio 17, 23, 24, 99, 100, *TM*
Neradhes (valley, stream) 103, 104, *105*
Nissi Beach **40-1**
Omodhos 26, 27, 33
Pafos (Paphos) 5, 32, 33, 34, 38, 44, 48, 49, 74, 78, **130**
town plan 10
Pakhna **26**, 27
Panagia Angeloktistos (church at Kiti) 38, 118, *119*, **120**
Panagia tou Araka (church near Lagoudhera) *64-5*, **65**
Pano Amiandos 36, 52, *56-7*
Pano Arkhimandrita 26, 33, 87, **88**, **89**, *90*
Pano Panagia 30
Pano Theletra 103, *105*
Paralimni 39, 40
Passia's Meadow (picnic site) 34
Pedhoulas **32**, 44
Pegia 22
Pegia Forest *92-3*, 86
Pera Pedi 16, 32, 33, *67*, **68**
Peristerona (near Lefkosia) 34, **35**
Perivolia 118, *119*, 120
Persephone Nature Trail 16, **52**, *56-7*
Petra tou Romiou (*see also* Aphrodite's Rocks) 26, 27, **cover**
Phasoula 33
Phini *56-7*
Phinikaria *108-9*, 110, 111, 112
Phrenaros 39, 40
Pissouri 27, 87
Pissouromouti (peak) 100, *TM*
Pittokopos 24, *82-3*
Platania 34
Platres 16, 32, 33, 34, 44, 48, *56-7*, 60, 62

Polis 22, 23, 44, 49, 96, *TM*
Pouziaris (plateau) *56-7*, 60, 61
Prodhromi 22, 23, *TM*
Prodhromos 33, 44, *56-7*, 62, 63
Profitis Ilias (church at Protaras) **39**, 40, *122-3*, 125, 126
Protaras (also called Fig Tree Bay) 40, 44, 121, *122-3*, 125, 126
Psilon Dhendron 16, 34, **35**, *56-7*, 60, 61
Pyrga 37, 38
Pyrgos tis Rigaenas 17, 98, **99**, 100, *TM*
Saittas 32, 33, 34
Selladi tou Stavrou Nature Trail 28, 69, *71*
Silikou *67*, **68**
Skoulli 22, 23
Smigies Nature Trail (and picnic site) **17**, 22, 24, 98, **99**, 100, *TM*
Statos 28, 31
Stavros tis Psokas 28, **29**, **69**, *69*, **70-1**
Stavros tou Agiasmati (church) *64-5*
Stavrouvouni (monastery) 18, 34, 36, 37, 38, 44, 49, *116*, **117**
Stroumbi 22, 25
Tala 74, *75*
Teisia tis Madaris Nature Trail *64-5*, 66
Temple of Apollo 27
Terra *101*, **102**
Throni 29, **30-1**
Trimiklini 34
Trooditissa (monastery) *56-7*, 62, **63**
Troodos (village) 15, 16, 33, 34, 50, 52, 53, *56-7*
(mountains) **1**, 5, 14, 15, 16, 32, 33, 44, 45, 48, 50, **51**, **53**, **54**, **55**, *56-7*, **58**, **61**, **63**
Xylophagou 39, 41
Xylotimbou (picnic site) 39, 40